THE BOOK OF GENESIS

SIDGWICK & JACKSON
LONDON

First published in Great Britain in 1984
by Sidgwick and Jackson Limited

ISBN: 0-283-99074-0

Edited and Produced by Nicky Hodge/Limbo Books Limited
Designed by David Fudger
Cover Photograph by Robert Ellis

Printed in Great Britain by R J Acford
for Sidgwick and Jackson Limited
1 Tavistock Chambers
Bloomsbury Way
London WC1A 2SG

Photographs supplied by
Jill Furmanovsky, London Features International, Michael Putland, Rex Features, Joe Bangay, Charisma Records, Photofeatures, Robert Ellis, Andy Hanson, Chris Walter, Terry Murden, Steve Emberton, Waring Abbott, Paul Canty, David Corio, Barry Wentzell, Ron Duggins, Barry Plummer, Gererd Mankowitz, Bill Smith and Dave Hill.

THE BOOK OF GENESIS

FROM INTERVIEWS WITH

HUGH FIELDER &
PHIL SUTCLIFFE

ACKNOWLEDGMENTS

Thank you Tony and Margaret Banks, Phil Collins and Jill, Mike and Angie Rutherford, Peter Gabriel, Steve Hackett, Anthony Phillips, Bill Bruford, Daryl Stuermer and Chester Thompson.

The company they keep — thank you Tony Smith, Gail Colson, Carol Willis, Norma and Andy Mackrill.

Invaluable background information — thank you Tony Stratton-Smith, Paul Conroy, Glen Colson, David Stopps, Jonathan King, Richard McPhail, Peter Thompson, Amando Gallo and Geoff Parkyn.

Inspiration and perspiration — thank you Nicky Hodge, Jill Chalk, Hilary Toovey, Lynne Shippam, Dave Fudger, Andrew Crilley, Peter Gerard Pearse, Lee Ellen Newman, Jill Furmanovsky, Ana, Gay Lee, Lesley, two Chloes and a Laurasauras.

CONTENTS

INTRODUCTION

I was never an ardent Genesis fan. I saw them once in 1971 at the Marquee and although I was stirred by their evocative music, I was put off by the fact that they seemed so earnest about what they were doing. Peter Gabriel's attempts to loosen things up only served to reinforce how stiff and awkward the others appeared.

This was supposedly the era when rock and roll was busy proving that it was more than mere entertainment. I was intrigued but, as I'd already been fooled once, going off in search of the lost chord with the Moody Blues, I was suspicious of another 'pomp rock' band.

I didn't see Genesis again with Gabriel although my younger brother was a fan and I occasionally listened to 'Nursery Cryme' or 'Foxtrot' when I went home at weekends.

In 1976, less than a year after I joined *Sounds*, I saw Genesis at the Hammersmith Odeon on their first tour without Gabriel. This time I was easily seduced. The rock theatre element had been supplanted by a stunning stage show that mirrored the music's powerful self-assurance.

It was rock and roll on a grand scale but without the indulgence that usually went with it. Genesis were concentrating hard on being a group while most of their contemporaries seemed to be concentrating hard on their egos.

A year later I wrote the first of several features on the band. By now they were distinctly unfashionable — branded as 'boring old farts' by a rock press eager to replace them with new heroes.

But I soon discovered that they were as unlike the ageing dinosaur bands who were clogging up the rock scene as they were to the abrasive young pretenders. Individually they came over as quiet and polite men and reticent to give their music as much significance as many of their dedicated followers did.

I found Genesis surprisingly easy to get on with. They didn't feel they had any kind of image to protect and were open-minded in conversation as long as you didn't deliberately put them on the defensive. They knew what they weren't and were almost apologetic about it. But they seemed to have an increasingly flexible sense of what they were, or could be.

By the end of the seventies Genesis had become a very successful band although they were seldom heard on the radio and almost never seen on TV. Their reputation was based on the distinguished musical trademarks they'd perfected for themselves within the 'progressive' style and the splendour and intensity of their live shows which were always extravagant without being either ostentatious or pretentious.

Musically I felt they were in danger of reaching a creative hiatus but, at the beginning of the eighties, they started stripping down their sound, deflating much of their musical pomposity and, at the same time, finding new challenges to explore.

The result was a series of hit singles that gave them mass popularity in Britain and America way beyond their large cult following. They achieved this without any noticeable compromise — indeed the only perceptible change I could detect was a more relaxed atmosphere between them.

Most bands struggle to develop creatively after a couple of albums. Only a handful can keep it up after half a dozen, and yet Genesis were evolving quite radically after a dozen. Indeed, not one of their albums can be considered an idle reproduction of it's predecessor — which is not to say that each one is necessarily better than the last.

A Genesis fan could bask in the knowledge that his group would always deliver to the limit of their ability and could touch emotions few other bands did.

I remember following a group of kids down from the balcony of the Dundee Caird Hall in 1980 after a concert. They were still reeling from the effects of 'Afterglow', a romantic anthem during which the hall had been bathed in purple light coming from behind the band, who appeared like fuzzy silhouettes amid the billowing smoke.

The kids were giggling self-consciously; their emotions weren't notably profound but they were embarrassingly hard to articulate. I watched that same stage-effect from all conceivable angles a dozen times that year and I got goosebumps down my neck every single time.

Genesis can maintain the same magnificent standard night after night because they hire the best road crew and the best lighting crew and, more important, look after them.

One of the crew once told me, "Nobody works for Led Zeppelin or ELO twice. They take the food away from the dressing-room if something goes wrong with the show and generally treat you like minions. But with Genesis you're regarded as an integral part of the operation. That's why we come running whenever they ask."

These most hardened of rock and roll professionals are not put off by Genesis' unconformity which occasionally reaches almost surreal heights of domesticity. At the same Dundee concert I watched Tony Banks and Mike Rutherford kiss their children goodnight by the side of the stage only ten seconds before they walked out to a full-throated roar of welcome from the audience.

They could indulge in such paternal pleasures without a hint of complacency creeping in. In the dressing-room immediately after the show, they discussed what went wrong before thinking about what went right.

Genesis are an insular band, partly by choice and partly by background. Yet when Phil Sutcliffe and I conducted the interviews for this book we were continually surprised by their candour and objectivity in looking back over their career. They were able to discuss the relationships in the band and their own contributions to it with a remarkable frankness that most 'rock stars' lack.

Their perspectives on the history of Genesis convinced me that they should tell the story in their own words. This book is simply the recollections of the people who have played in Genesis (bar the first two or three drummers and a temporary guitarist).

It is not an 'official' biography and neither does it claim to be 'fully comprehensive'. Amando Gallo has already presented an authoritative account of their career in *Genesis — I Know What I Like* (currently out of print), while Geoff Parkyn's *Genesis — An Illustrated Discography* (Omnibus) will tell you where to find 'Twilight Alehouse' and how many other albums Phil Collins has played on. The individual solo careers have not been covered because I soon realised that they would need a book to themselves.

I think *The Book Of Genesis* will appeal not only to Genesis followers, but also to your average rock and roll fan curious about what makes a band tick.

I have deliberately passed no comment or judgement on their quotes. That's the prerogative of the reader.

HUGH FIELDER, 1984

1950-1969

- **Tony Banks, born March 1950 in East Hoathly, Sussex.**
- **Peter Gabriel, born February 1950 in Woking, Surrey.**
- **Mike Rutherford, born October 1950 in Guildford, Surrey.**
- **Anthony Phillips, born December 1951 in Putney, South London.**

TONY: I was born in East Hoathly which is about 15 miles from Brighton — and then we moved when I was about 11 to a place which was nearer to Hastings.

My father was a teacher. He used to get children through the Common Entrance examination which is what you have to take to get into public school. By cramming them effectively he'd get a pretty good success rate out of rather poor quality material. He liked teaching, and I think he liked being at home, you know, because he was able to do this all from where we lived.

I was quite fussy, I suppose as a child. On my very first day at prep school I sat staring at a bowl of porridge right up until lunchtime. I never liked porridge the whole time I was there and I was there for about six years. Some days it was just more than I could bear and, as there were various loose floorboards in the dining room, I used to lift them up when everyone had gone, and throw the porridge down.

●PETER: My father was born into a family of timber merchants — Gabriel, Wade and English. Most of the family members — particularly the duds — had safe jobs with the family firm. My father was much more of a thinker than the rest of them and more inclined towards scientific things. He studied at the University of London and became an electrical engineer. He was involved with the development of radar flight simulators and he designed a cable TV system called Dial-A-Programme, which was, I believe, the first operating TV system using fibre optics.

My childhood was spent playing with animals and lots of little girls. I had a very liberated sex life, between the ages of 4 and 7, which I never really recovered from.

My mother's family were all musical, a very Victorian family with five sisters, all of whom would play different instruments and sing together on musical evenings. I used to hate it as a teenager but, I think, some of it must have sunk in. Around Christmas time, there always

REX FEATURES

□ *Tony and Benjamin.*

MICHAEL PUTLAND/LFI

□*Peter, 1973.*

used to be a collection of aunts gathering around the grand piano.

There were times when I would be left to my own devices. My mother and sister were both into riding and pony clubs. This didn't appeal to me, so I would find myself wandering around in a world of my own. That's probably when I started my preoccupation with fantasy.

I think I found it quite easy to get on with other kids. I wasn't a macho, sporty male. I would prefer doctors and nurses with the girls behind the flower beds to cowboys and indians.

My grandfather's house at Cox Hill which later became an ashram, was the inspiration for 'Musical Box'. There was a formal garden there with a croquet lawn, goldfish pond, rose garden, squash court and a greenhouse, surrounded by vines and fig trees. There was also a shed where my grandfather kept various bits of exercising equipment. Inside this shed was a wooden railway track, which was a fantastic toy. It was probably very small, but I remember it as being very big. There were lots of privet hedges and places to get lost.

However I felt that beneath the formalised structure of all this Victoriana, there was an underlying violence which I tried to get across in the song.

I went to nursery school about 200 yards down the road, then there was a prep school which was in the other direction, towards Woking. That was where most of the flower-bed activities took place. And then, just a little further down the hill was St Andrews School for boys. I boarded there for my last year, which was a relatively peaceful transition for me as I could cycle home for weekends.

There used to be boys from the nearby state schools who would hide in the gorse bushes and beat us up and take our bicycles. So we ended up forming a gang, as a means of self-defence. We'd gradually gather, and by the time we got within a mile of the school, there were about fifteen boys, all cycling together. This meant that there was a good chance you could outnumber the opposition! I hate the class system, and I think that the school system is one of the most effective means by which this country perpetuates its class divisions.

●MIKE: My father was in the Navy and I was brought up at various naval establishments. One was in Portsmouth — a place called Whale Island. Although I never actually thought about joining the Navy, I did take it quite seriously at one point. My father never suggested it, but I suppose it came about as a result of my background.

When I was about five, my father left the Navy and we moved up to Cheshire. At the age of 7, I went off to prep school, which was in the Wirral, Cheshire. Boarding at the age of 7 was really terrifying. I would never send any of my kids to board at that age.

I was a fairly quiet, shy little boy, who was suddenly thrown in at the deep end...I actually got to school a day late. I locked myself in the lavatory, and they couldn't get me out!

I guess my musical career started when I was about 8. I was into Cliff at that time. My sister was buying records — Elvis, Cliff and the Shads. I listened and really liked what I heard and I decided I particularly liked the guitar. It had a nice symmetrical shape.

After pestering my parents they bought me a classical guitar. I bought Bert Weedon's *Play in a Day*. There was no-one at school to teach me but I picked up a few basic chords and listened to the radio.

To be honest, I wish I'd had lessons in those days. I learnt a few Cliff songs and gave my first public performance. God, I must have been brave! I suppose I was about 10. It was a school concert, I got up and sang 'Travellin' Light' and 'Michael Row The Boat Ashore'.

I couldn't really tune the guitar — I hadn't mastered that yet. There was a teacher who tuned it for me on the morning of the show. However, by the time I actually had to go on stage, it had gone badly out of tune. I was at least musical enough to know it was out. I battled through, and it went down a bomb. I really don't know why, it must have sounded awful. So that was my first public appearance.

A guy called Dimitri arrived at my prep school who played guitar as well. We both bought our little amps, and went electric.

I remember going into a shop in Manchester without actually realising that electric guitars were any different. I didn't know they had amplifiers and stuff. You know the cartoons they sometimes have in the paper where there's this guy — usually a long haired guy — playing his guitar attached to a plug that goes into the wall. The cartoon would show Dad

REX FEATURES

□ *Mike and Kate.*

complaining about the noise and ripping the plug out of the socket.

Well, I went into this shop and said "I would like an electric guitar." The man said, "What kind of amp would you like?" And I said, "I don't want an amp — I want an electric guitar, I don't need an amplifier. What do I need an amplifier for?"

It was very embarrassing. He broke it to me. In the end, I bought a Hofner, a semi-acoustic one with F holes in it, and a Selmer Little Giant amplifier.

It was still going when we made the first album. It blasted the house and my father would go outside and worry that it would fall down.

● ANT: I was brought up in Putney, South London. My father was a merchant banker — or he *was* a merchant banker. He's now a retired merchant banker — a very successful, retired merchant banker.

I went away to boarding school when I was 8, to Hindhead in Surrey. I picked up a guitar there at the age of 11. That was in the era of Hank and the Shadows. It was great. I'll always remember playing 'Foot Tapper' and stuff like that on a small acoustic guitar.

We had this school group with all sorts of guys that couldn't play anything. There was a bloke called Sid who used to be in D Seventh for every single song, and a drummer called Bonehead, who literally used to attack the drums. There was no question of rhythm.

We were called the Spiders. There was another slightly famous group from Liverpool, just starting out around then. And we thought the Spiders was a very original name!

■ **Charterhouse, near Godalming, Surrey, is one of England's archetypal public schools. Tony and Peter started there at the age of 13, in September 1963. Mike followed in September 1964 and Ant in April 1965.**

● PETER: Going to Charterhouse was traumatic. I remember the first night. There were no curtains in the dormitory and it was very bleak and cold. I'd been used to living in the country; even the prep school had been very quiet at night-time. The school building was on a hill at the edge of the road and, with no curtains, car headlights used to shine up through the windows. They looked like anti-aircraft lights.

It was a real wrench feeling that I'd been thrown into this cold, merciless environment. And, at the time, Charterhouse still had remnants of *Tom Brown's School Days*. There were monitors beating fags and a lot of structured cruelty within the system. It was very definitely a shock.

You were taught to be leaders of men. You had the feeling that you were being trained as a race apart. You were not encouraged to mix with the boys in the town. All sorts of shocking, ideological stuff was just pumped into you.

I suppose it gave us, as insecure teenagers some kind of foothold with which to take on 'life' — at that age you aren't about to question things that are giving you some sort of support.

● MIKE: I arrived there quite happy. But then I had a terrible time, mainly because I had a rather strange housemaster. It's funny how certain people in your life never leave you. If he opened that door now and said, "Rutherford, what have you been doing?" I think I'd probably fall over or start shaking. He was an odd individual, he was convinced the revolution was going to start in his particular house.

I was never particularly naughty, but I got on the wrong side of him all the way down the line; even when I spent a couple of terms trying to be really good. He and I were fireworks. I even remember throwing a telephone at him at the end.

This guy banned me from playing the guitar for my entire time at Charterhouse, except for maybe a year, I don't know why, really. I think he saw the guitar as a symbol of the revolution.

● ANT: In your first year there was only one room you could basically inhabit, and you had to sit at tables. You couldn't sit on a chair away from the table; you certainly couldn't sit on a window sill in your first year. You even had to walk round the table a certain way; really petty things which had no basis in common sense were enforced, merely to perpetuate a kind of caste system.

We were given a terribly hard time. If anybody in a band did badly in class, he wasn't allowed to play the guitar for two weeks. The teachers were worried because they saw rebellion and anarchy brewing up, and, as a result, they over-reacted. They also saw clothes they hadn't seen before, and they associated them with chaos. There were always a lot of people hanging round the bands — they did tend to attract the ne'er-do-wells.

● TONY: I got a scholarship to Charterhouse. And I steadily went downhill academically for about the next 2 or 3 years. I really didn't like it there at all. I enjoyed my later years because I was getting much more involved in music.

I'd been learning classical music but, as time went on, I started to get into playing with other people, particularly with Peter. We used to play together a lot in our spare time.

■ **Tony and Peter soon became friends, while Mike teamed up with Ant. They were drawn together by a fascination with the rock music explosion of the Sixties as well as a passing interest in school hymns.**

DAVID HILL/LFI

□*Ant, 1973.*

● PETER: Tony was a bit edgy. I felt I had a hard time socialising but I think he had an even harder time. I think that really, my friendship with Tony developed out of a mutual interest in the piano.

As soon as the games period finished we would have a fight for access to the piano. Sometimes this would mean clambering through the food hatch in order to beat the person running through the door. It was that critical.

● TONY: My mother had wanted me to take piano lessons and I started them at the age of 7. To be honest, I don't know how much I really enjoyed them. I wasn't terribly good, for a start, as I never found it easy to read music. I was pretty disillusioned by the time I got to Charterhouse and I had a really bad teacher when I first went there. He kept on giving me pieces of music that just didn't interest me until he gave up.

In the end, I swapped to another teacher who gave me various pieces of music that I wanted to learn. Rachmaninov's first prelude was one of them because I'd heard other people playing it and I knew that it was fairly simple. And, after that, there were quite a few others.

I remember the first song I ever worked out on the piano was 'Sheila' by Tommy Roe which was very simple — three chords, I think. And slowly I developed the way I played other people's songs.

● PETER: The first song I wrote was called 'Sammy The Slug'. I was about 13. I don't think it was particularly memorable! So the first topic that I decided I was capable of writing about was slugs.

● TONY: Pete and I were friends and we used to work things out together. He used to have the sheet music for various pieces that I'd never actually heard of and I quite enjoyed playing along with him. We were close friends the whole time we were at school together but it wasn't until people like Otis Redding that we found that we really liked the same kind of music. 'I Put A Spell On You' was another song that we both liked a lot.

Obviously when you are playing with one person for quite a lot of the time you start to write things together. You try chords that other people haven't used.

My first compositions tended to be overcomplex because I was trying to do everything that everyone else hadn't done. Then we started to do things together and while we were still at school, we actually wrote one or two songs, which appeared on 'From Genesis To Revelation'.

● PETER: I think Tony and I were beginning to build up a rapport of sorts. There were definitely things about each other's early musical offerings that we didn't like. But there were many elements that we did like and so we concentrated on them. I think that it was when we started to write songs together that we thought we might get them recorded.

So, on the one hand, Tony and I were thinking of being song writers, whereas Mike and Ant were really into playing in a group and doing Stones imitations at parties...I also wanted to play the drums, but not so much with this kind of material.

I had definitely got into beat music and soul music in my first few years at Charterhouse. I think it was a sort of express train into the heart. These people were singing as if they meant it. Most of the shit one heard on the radio had no real feeling behind it, like so much pop music. With soul singers there's a really powerful emotion there — whether they mean the words or not.

I remember the billiard room vividly; it was the only place that we could play music. It had this really beaten up, old Dansette record player in a wooden cabinet. You could only play it for about an hour and a half every day.

I used to take my Otis Redding records in there and turn them up full volume and dance until I was in a frenzied sweat. This ritual gave me an immense feeling of relief.

I used to play drums in a dance band called M'Lords and then in a soul band called the Spoken Word. I wanted to be a drummer at that point, but at the same time, I realised that I also wanted to write songs.

I virtually had to start my piano playing again from scratch, which is why, I think, I bought the sheet music. Tony was always skint, I mean, you could never get him to buy anything. I wasn't given much money, but I suppose I probably had more than he did.

The first album I had was the Beatles' first album. I can remember exactly where I was when I first heard 'Love Me Do'. There are probably ten records where I can recall the emotional excitement of hearing something which was new, earthy and gutsy. Like Nina Simone's 'I Put A Spell On You' for example.

Hymns were also a big musical influence on me but only at school. In church I always felt that they were played too slow. I also hated the ritual of church-going.

At school, you knew no-one gave a damn about the religious aspect of hymns, they were just singing the tunes that they liked. The ones that we all liked, we would really belt out. It was a bit like singing at a football match. I still think that good hymns have some of the best melodies that have ever been written.

● MIKE: I was in the choir when I first arrived at Charterhouse, but it actually became so demanding time-wise that I couldn't keep it up. They had a wonderful modern hymn book at Charterhouse, and we sang fantastic hymns made up largely of very simple chord changes.

Very often I enjoyed the musical side of chapel — the religious side I think would put anyone off.

● TONY: I loved the sound of the organ and the only thing I enjoyed about chapel was when we sang a nice hymn. Sometimes, after the service on Sundays, they would play a piece like Bach's 'Toccata And Fugue' on the organ, which sounded tremendous.

● PETER: From about 15 onwards, I began to get a sense of idealism from reading things that introduced me to new points of view. Then, towards the end of my time at school, came the flower-power era and all the great breakthroughs that came with it — the Beatles, drugs, long hair. It was all tremendously exciting to observe from this Colditz in the middle of suburbia. And occasionally I would sneak away and go to clubs like Middle Earth in London.

● ANT: Peter was into all sorts of things. Peter was a clever boy. He had some hats made by Dunns. Have you ever heard about Peter's hats? Everyone used to buy his hats. He also used to dye everybody's teeshirts for them at Charterhouse. Our white shirts became turquoise. A colourful man, Peter. He always had a lot of creative ideas.

● PETER: There was this whole exciting world of hippies and Carnaby Street and *Rave* magazine that I could only be part of during the school holidays. There was no way that our music was touching any of this. The clothes seemed to offer a way in.

I found this old hat in my grandfather's dressing-up box. I took it round all sorts of different shops in London to see if I could find a hat manufacturer, and ended up at Dunn and Co in Piccadilly. I don't know what they must have thought when they saw this spotty-looking schoolboy walking in with this strange hat. I think the old guy, who was running the place, was quite amused by it.

They took it in and had a look at it and sent it round to their factory, where they said that they could make them.

I wanted bright colours so they had them done in pinks and purples and yellows and greens and oranges — all sorts of very loud, gaudy colours. And then, I had to take them round boutiques to try and flog them.

One of the most exciting moments of my childhood was coming home from school, and switching on *Juke Box Jury* to see Marianne Faithfull wearing one of my hats. I nearly wet myself!

I also used to try and increase my pocket money at school by dyeing people's shirts for 10p a go, and this got me into a certain amount of trouble because they went into the wash with the cricket whites, which then came out pink or green! So that came to a halt.

There was this very naive fantasy going round at the time that a revolution, a sudden surge of idealism, was going to come through the music and the clothes — indeed through youth.

I remember when they made the first worldwide TV satellite link, with the Beatles singing 'All You Need Is Love'. It felt like, "We've made it". Very naive stuff, but I was very excited. I felt part of the generation. It was a really exciting thing to watch and feel — even if you were just a spectator, which I was. I was just a weekend hippy.

● MIKE: The social upheaval around the time of the Beatles, the Animals and all the rest didn't register. I knew that it was happening, but it meant absolutely nothing. All that really mattered was the music and how it affected me and how excited I was by it.

All that stuff about people's background — where they came from or where I came from for that matter — was pretty irrelevant as far as I was concerned. I would have happily changed places with anyone at the time.

The fact that we all came from that background, however, might have affected our songwriting, as we started off writing songs that were inspired more by literature and fantasy, than by sex and drugs. That was because we were all so shy. Pete was the bravest. You do come out of public school feeling very insecure and unsure with girls. It takes about 10 years to get over that I think!

My most enjoyable part of the day, apart from the group, was when I used to go off with a friend called Richard Pickett after lunch. We used to finish lunch about 1.30, and until 2.00, we were free. We used to bicycle down to the pub, have a couple of gins and a pie. It was a means of escapism even if only for half an hour. I also kept a motorbike in the pub — which was highly illegal. We used to go off for the odd evening and occasionally up to town — where I first saw the Cream — and come back very late. I was actually quite naughty, but I never got caught for anything serious — just minor petty things, like being in the wrong place at the wrong time.

● PETER: I remember that Tony and I were both lectured about mixing with 'undesirable elements' as our housemaster called them. This included 'Rutherford', but not Ant. Ant was very good at cricket, and our housemaster was a real cricket fan. Even though Ant did have these slight tendencies for disreputable behaviour, all was recovered on the cricket pitch.

■ **Ant formed the Anon soon after arriving at Charterhouse. When they played a school concert in July 1966 Ant also performed with the Garden Wall, an occasional combo featuring Tony on offstage grand piano, Peter on vocals, with kaftan and rose petals, and drummer Chris Stewart. Afterwards, the writing partnerships of Ant and Mike and Peter and Tony moved closer together and a demo tape was made.**

● MIKE: Basically my first connection with 'the group' was meeting Ant. He seemed to be an incredibly competent guitarist. He'd had lessons, knew more chords than I did, and he could actually work out the chords to the songs.

I didn't really know Pete and Tony, I only knew of them.

● ANT: The first group at Charterhouse was called the Anon, it included Mike but none of the other Genesis members. At that time we were just doing Stones numbers. These really caught the imagination of the school and we did some beat concerts.

I had carried on the group with Rivers Job on bass from prep school. Richard McPhail, who later worked for Genesis, was our singer; he was the sort of Mick Jagger — I was the Keith Richards. Mike came into it as rhythm guitarist; he was also lead vocalist at one point. We had a very good drummer called Rob Tyrell.

We played together for about a year and a half, having a great time. Then the blues boom came along, and a lot of people got sucked into that, and things changed. People were buying motorbikes and stuff. Everything sort of fragmented.

By that stage, I was old enough to be able to talk to Peter Gabriel and Tony Banks, who were 2 years older than me. The age difference had meant they were sort of distant, lofty individuals. Peter was a very strange creature. He was very large, in fact he was like a barrel in those days. He was always very quiet. He's still quiet. He was a drummer to start with. I remember trying to borrow his drums once, and he was very worried about it. He came along and sat through the whole thing, nervously looking at his drums.

He was so meticulous about the way the kit was put together and taken apart again.

I used to listen to Tony playing Beatles songs on the piano and I would strum along with the guitar. That's how we really began. Gradually I became aware of this strange individual who would occasionally stand on the dining room table and sing — this was Peter.

● MIKE: The Garden Wall started a bit later, because Ant was put into the same house as Pete and Tony. There were a couple of concerts at which both bands played. By then, I think, I had been banned from playing the guitar so I couldn't play in the end of term concerts.

● TONY: The Garden Wall. Just a name really. I don't know where it came from. Pete and I had been playing together and there was this trumpet player called Johnny Trapman who wanted to form a group and so we all got together. Chris Stewart came in on drums. He ended up in the first Genesis line-up.

Ant was the only guitarist in the school really, which meant he ended up playing guitar. He also had his own amp which was why he was so sought after.

Ant was also quite good. He could play like Keith Richards. Originally — funnily enough — our idea had been to play something closer to the blues.

● ANT: The end of term concert was a sort of Anon benefit. The Anon were the big act. At this stage, there was no Genesis; it was just Peter and Tony. In fact, I don't even think Mike played. I think he was off with the drinkers; he had a spell of being 'one of the lads'.

It was a great concert because it was totally unrehearsed. Tony was playing the piano which nobody could hear the whole way through. We had a drummer called Chris Stewart, who was an excellent guy, but he used to make the most terrible faces when he played.

We did this 12-bar blues to start with, which just went on and on; for these were the days when the singer used to turn round and wave his hand to stop the drummer. Pete kept turning round at the end of each cycle to find that Chris was making a face in the other direction, so we just kept going, time after time. It got so embarrassing.

In the end the whole thing ground to a halt because Richard McPhail had got up to announce one of the songs. This rather poofy music master had said that there should be no announcements because you didn't have them at classical concerts.

During the changeover of instruments there was a terrible silence, and Richard, with great presence of mind had said "Sorry folks, it's all part of the act. The next number we're going to do is one of our own compositions." Thirty seconds into the song the music master was on the side of the stage shouting "Stop! It's got to stop!" And the concert was stopped in an uproar, because we had made an announcement!

● PETER: Playing in the band was more Mike and Ant's thing at that time. I was just an afterthought, I think. Tony was originally going to play keyboards, and then he used that as a wedge to get one or two of our songs onto a tape that was done in Chiswick at a friend called Brian Roberts' studio.

Richard McPhail, who later became our tour manager, was really the main singer, and he was a better singer and performer than I was at the time. But then the others seemed to prefer my voice to Richard's. Or maybe Tony just wheedled me in; I can't remember.

● MIKE: Pete came along just to have a look and do a bit of singing. Tony wanted him to sing but I had never heard him before. Ant was keen to sing at the time, although his voice was actually as bad as mine. The first thing Pete sang was 'She's Beautiful'. It sounded great — a real voice. We did some rehearsing in one of the classrooms.

It was only as we were leaving school that we started to get it together. I think Pete and Ant were still there. I had left and Tony had gone to university. And then Pete went to a crammer in London. It was at that point that we really started to take it seriously.

REX FEATURES

□ *Phil and Simon.*

Ant and I had been doing Stones' songs, and then we got into the blues — John Mayall and Clapton etc. That's when I first started to go and see gigs. I can't remember what sparked it off but the blues suddenly went right out of the window, and we started writing our own stuff.

●TONY: Blues music was very easy to do. There were an awful lot of bands who just went out and played endless 12-bars. I wanted to be more original than that. At the time we got together, classical music hadn't really been used much in rock. The idea of using pianos was something that hadn't been done before and I felt it was an interesting area to explore.

●MIKE: Initially Ant and I wrote together, just as Tony and Pete were doing. The songs on the first album, 'Genesis to Revelation', were mainly written by either of the two pairs, although there were a couple that we all collaborated on — 'In The Beginning' and 'The Conqueror'.

●ANT: Mike and I were constantly trying to write our own stuff. We were also doing demos at Brian Roberts' studio in Chiswick. One day I asked Tony to come up and play some keyboards. Tony then asked if his mate, Pete, could come along and if they could record one song of their own.

And, of course, their song was far better than any of ours. Ours were desperate. I remember too that Pete used to sweat an incredible amount in those days. I don't know why this all comes back to me! Anyway their song was called 'She's Beautiful' which eventually became 'The Serpent' on 'From Genesis To Revelation'.

■**The demo tape was passed to Old Carthusian Jonathan King, rising young Turk of the pop business, who signed Peter, Tony, Mike, Ant and Chris to Decca Records and gave them their name. After two unsuccessful recording sessions Peter and Tony wrote a song specifically to please King. 'The Silent Sun' was released as a single in February 1968 but failed to bring instant stardom, as did a second single, 'A Winter's Tale', in May 1968. Undeterred and with a new drummer, John Silver, they recorded an 'ambitious' concept album in a day. 'From Genesis To Revelation' was released in March 1969 to minimal interest.**

●ANT: Jonathan King came down to Charterhouse. It must have been early summer '67. A friend of ours called John Alexander was pushed towards King with this tape — we were all too scared.

He liked it and we signed a publishing contract for £40 for four songs — £10 each advance. We really thought that was a lot of money. It probably was quite a lot in those days.

●PETER: We were using the old boy network. And I think, at that time, King seemed quite happy to use the young boy network. He gave us some money to experiment with and told us to produce a demo.

He was interested, and I would have to go down to the phone box out of school on the hill, and struggle with my coins and the pip box, to try and locate this person from the pop business. At that point, everyone who was involved with the music business was regarded with suspicion, including King.

●TONY: We were sixteen, maybe seventeen. We just saw the dotted line. Here was the big man, Jonathan King from London. He'd even had a hit record.

We thought we were stars; we thought we'd made it at that point and we hadn't even read the contract. We just signed it.

●PETER: We talked about a name for the group with King. His first suggestion, which the rest of the band have forgotten although I haven't, was Gabriel's Angels — which appealed to me! Somehow this didn't seem to register with the others.

King actually suggested it again when we found that there was another band called Genesis in America, and we were considering a name change. I think his thinking was that some of the stuff was influenced by hymns, and so this new name suggested an absurd, naive innocence.

All the original demos that King had heard were with acoustic instruments, which he thought gave us quite a novel sound. He's shrewd — King — and much better at spotting hits than making them and he came up with quite a lot of outrageous ideas for us. He was an interesting person to be dealing with.

●TONY: We did a couple of tapes which King didn't like and so, in desperation, Peter and I wrote 'Silent Sun' because we wanted something that would recapture his interest. Yes, we really did calculate it like that. We thought, "Well, who does he like?" and came up with the Bee Gees. The song we really liked by the Bee Gees at that time was 'To Love Somebody'. So we wrote a song like that and he loved it. He thought it was good enough for a single.

●PETER: I do remember that we tried to write something that sounded like a Bee Gees ballad. I tried to sing a little bit like Robin Gibb on the second verse of 'Silent Sun'. I'm sure we would have denied it at the time, as we have denied other influences at later stages. Anyway it worked and it was put out as a single.

Another of my highlights was the first time I saw Genesis in print in an advert in the *Record*

Mirror, which was then partly owned by Decca Records. It only took up about a sixteenth of a page, but to see it in print was very exciting.

●ANT: 'Silent Sun' was quite a nice song although I never liked it to start with. I thought Peter and Tony had sold out — it was all just a deliberate build-up to the chorus. But it wasn't really like that at all.

●MIKE: I remember hearing 'Silent Sun' on the Kenny Everett Show, it was the first song he played that Sunday morning. I was at Ant's house and it was such a buzz!

It got quite a lot of plays, and we thought "Here we go!." We even went out and bought our gear for *Top of the Pops* — black and white. I had black trousers and a white jacket; Tony had the reverse. Thank goodness nothing happened, because I don't think we'd have got anywhere if we'd had a hit. It would have finished us off, we were so inexperienced and we wouldn't have been able to cope.

●TONY: At the time, Jonathan King had an ITV show called *Good Evening* — which we assumed we'd get on but we never did, because he couldn't swing it. I think it's just as well we didn't get on TV or have a success with that record because it might well have stopped us developing.

And then after a second, equally unsuccessful single called 'A Winter's Tale', King suggested we did an album. We actually thought that the music we were writing was more suitable for an album. However, the album got about the same interest as the singles — not very much at all.

We also released another single off the album called 'Where The Sour Turns To Sweet'. I remember accosting Tony Blackburn in the street and telling him to play it. I actually said to him "Well, don't play the A-side, play the other side," which was called 'In Hiding'. It was a very embarrassing situation looking back on it. But at the time, Tony Blackburn was important enough for us to do that. This was quite a while ago.

●PETER: 'From Genesis To Revelation' was supposed to be the history of the universe, altogether a very duff concept. Listening to it now — I think there are some things that showed we had melody-writing potential. That's about all I can say. I think Ant was the best songwriter of us all at that point. Tony did some good melodies, but they were a bit stiff.

We recorded 'From Genesis To Revelation' in a day, and by the time I got to 'In The Wilderness' which was the most demanding vocal performance, it was pitched above my range. You could hear this desperate sort of retching noise as I struggled for the high notes. I had to keep taking showers, anything to try and keep me awake.

●TONY: The string arrangements on 'Silent Sun' had been quite successful. The strings and brass on the album were also pretty good as well. The real problem on the album was the production. Again it was done very fast. We were around for some of it, but we didn't have a clue about producing and so we left it up to Jonathan King. An awful lot of things got completely missed out. Some of the songs have got totally the wrong feel because of the bias of the mix.

The pastoral songs worked alright but the more aggressive songs really didn't come across that well, the one exception perhaps being 'In The Wilderness' which I think has got a bit of aggression to it. It's far and away the best track on the album. I don't think there's anything else to touch it.

●ANT: They stuck the strings on and then there was this dreadful business of the stereo mix. All the power of the track went down the tube on the left channel, and there was this dry nothing going on, on the right. I hated it.

I remember storming out of the session, suddenly the whole thing — this dream of a great album — had crumbled. I remember that when 'From Genesis To Revelation' came out, I really didn't want to know.

This thing about being able to play our instruments properly was a bit of a fallacy. Although Tony was proficient as a keyboard player and I was a reasonable guitarist — perhaps a bit coarse — Mike really couldn't play very much during the early era. The playing on 'From Genesis To Revelation' was pretty naff. After that, Mike turned from a very ordinary bass and rhythm guitarist, into a very good bassist in about nine months.

●MIKE: Jonathan King was a very valuable person, I think, because he gave us a unique opportunity. In those days for a bunch of unprofessional guys still at school to have been able to make a whole album was very unusual. Nowadays it's a lot easier to go into a studio to make an album if you are a new group. But in those days — '68/'69 — it didn't happen that way. Getting to do that was obviously a big thing because it whetted our appetites, and we began to get excited about recording techniques. Although it was exciting, it was also hard work and dissatisfying artistically because the songs didn't come out quite as we'd wanted them to. But it did give us a glimpse of what we thought we could do.

King was the kind of guy who got very excited about something and then he would go off and do something else. At any one time there'd be a project which was his baby, and for a while we were.

When he went off to do other things we were not so productive. Finally we lied and said we'd split up. He let us go, and we reformed a month later.

1969-1970

While Tony and Peter wavered, Ant and Mike's writing partnership was prolific and in September 1969, Genesis 'turned professional' with their third drummer, John Mayhew. In a cottage found for them by school friend/road manager Richard McPhail they worked up a new set of songs.

● ANT: It all got a bit tense, really, after 'From Genesis To Revelation' came out. There was no direction. We didn't know quite what we were doing.

We started off by rehearsing, and I pushed it in the wrong direction — some electric stuff which wasn't very good. In particular I remember Tony hated playing the organ, he used to call it a 'box of tricks'. He was very much a pianist, and didn't like it at all.

It was a very depressing time, really. Tony was at university, and had to decide whether he was to take a year off. That questioned our commitment and acted as a spur to the rest of us. I remember things being at such a low ebb that I really wasn't sure what to do. Mike and I had a massive burst of inspiration as far as our writing was concerned and had hit upon what I thought was a reasonably original style — this 12-string stuff. The other two had sort of drifted apart at that point for various different reasons, and didn't produce very much, but we were writing stacks and stacks of stuff.

There had been a six month period where I just couldn't get a song through the 'committee'. Then things started to change. It was partly a move towards the acoustic guitar, I think, that did it. I wrote 'Visions Of Angels' very early in 1968. And things got better after that.

● TONY: By this time John Silver said he was definitely going to leave. At one point, I also announced that I was going to quit and then I changed my mind. I was enjoying it too much.

There was one particular song we used to play which never ended up on any album or anything. It was called 'Pacidy'. I remember playing it at one of the various places we used for rehearsals — mainly friends' houses — and I just thought that this was something that I didn't want to give up. It was too good, you know.

After I had made the decision to stay, I had to persuade Pete too. Both of us had cold feet as to whether it was the right thing or not — particularly as in my case, it meant leaving university.

It was made easier for me when the universi-

□ *Gabriel's Angels 1968 — Ant, Mike, Tony, Peter and Chris.*

ty said they would give me a year off, so I could delay the real decision until after I'd had a chance to see what was going on.

Peter decided to stay, on condition that we made a tape to send around to see if we got any real interest. So we made a tape, played it around, got a real stone wall reaction, and he stayed!

I had no idea where I wanted to be as a result of it all. The main pull in the other direction was just the sheer fact of what I was expected to do. The last thing that was expected of me was to be a rock musician. It was virtually unheard of for people from my sort of background then. It was a difficult decision but in a sense, I always rather liked that aspect of it. I like doing the opposite of what is expected of me, and that was one way of doing it I suppose.

● PETER: I'd got a place at the London School of Film Technique. At that time I quite fancied being a film director.

I also auditioned for a part in the film *If....* I got past the first audition and went to do a reading. There were about eight major parts in the film and I was up for one of them.

I was on the 'maybe' list but then I started saying that I was in a band, that I wasn't sure if I could do this or that, that it depended on our records, and that I may want to go to film school, etc. At that point, they said, "Either you go for it, or you don't." And so, I said, "OK. Well, I don't." But it was still exciting, just to get a taste of it.

MIKE: I never had any doubts that the band was going to play professionally. I thought maybe I would do this for a couple of years. I never thought whether I was going to be a success. I mean, I thought I was, but then I never thought any further than that; at what level or when it might happen. I just thought "Right, this is what I'm going to do." I became quite determined about it from then on.

● TONY: I think Ant was probably the most important member during this early period — he was the one who held us together. He and Mike used to play stuff on their 12-string guitars which, to me, sounded totally unlike anything I'd heard before.

They wanted to try playing on stage but I don't think Peter and I were too enamoured of the idea.

● ANT: John Silver had been our drummer on 'From Genesis To Revelation', after which he'd gone off to an American university. He came back the following summer and was presented with a semi-ultimatum, "Are you going to play with us, or not?" He decided to go back to university.

We then started auditioning for drummers. Eventually we got hold of this guy called John

Mayhew. It was always a bit difficult, because I think he did feel there was a class barrier between us.

I was never aware of it; it was always other people who brought it up. We were called 'snotty-nosed bastards', once, apparently by some guy at Leicester University. Maybe we were. Anyway, John definitely felt it and never quite integrated into the group. I think one or two of us must have been a bit formidable at times, for him, really — looking back on it.

● MIKE: Richard McPhail provided the most amazing cottage — a fantastic place, outside Dorking, in the woods. An ideal situation. We moved in, and started writing and we must have been writing for at least three or four months before we actually started gigs.

We just went on and on writing. We'd get up in the morning, have our breakfast and go straight in there. We'd rehearse from ten in the morning, break for lunch then maybe go for a walk in the afternoon.

We never took time off to go and see movies or anything — we were far too intense to enjoy ourselves. We'd stay up until about three in the morning.

God, it was deafening, too, you know. We were in this small room, and by the time we'd turned the gear off in the evening, our ears were ringing. It was a valuable time though, as we actually started to play our instruments properly as well as learning how to write together. It was a very prolific time indeed — we wrote 'The Knife' and 'Stagnation' and 'White Mountain' and 'Vision Of Angels', and all sorts of songs there.

I look upon that time as the point at which we actually became a band.

● ANT: The whole cottage experience was rather silly. It did turn four or five raw musicians into a fully-fledged band, but I think, looking back on it, it really needn't have been done like that.

The idea that we would all live together in the same place 24 hours a day and still get on well was really so illusory as to be ridiculous.

It made the band, but I have thought since that if we had disciplined ourselves for six or seven hours each day we would have achieved the same thing with far less aggravation.

● TONY: We really got on top of each other whilst we were at the cottage. We always used to argue a lot in those early days. It seemed to be part of the creative process.

We used to care so much about each bit, you know, like whether that beat should be advanced or scrapped or something. You could loose sleep over it, I mean, it was that important.

● PETER: Tony and I were the most forceful characters when it came to making big decisions although Ant would stand guard over certain areas of the music and refuse to be moved. Ant was always much less interested in the live side of it.

When arguments arose over band policy, I remember I used to try and drop ideas for Tony to adopt, so that they became his ideas, or shared ideas.

● ANT: None of us were very good at talking. If there were problems, we were more likely to go off to a corner of the room and sit and think about it, as opposed to actually confronting somebody.

It got to the stage where I wasn't really communicating with anybody that well. It was, I suppose, inevitable because we were all so serious about music. I think it could have been a lot healthier if we'd just been a little bit more sensible. We were all so young.

Mike was pretty much as you find him today. Very friendly, charming, a bit of a lad. Peter was quiet, sincere, very kind, but always a little bit distant. Tony was quite insular — he could be very outward-going and very friendly, but he could also be very quiet and moody.

● MIKE: We all used to storm off; Pete and I were the only two that had girlfriends, which made it hard as we had another life outside the band.

I remember Pete walking out, he went up the road in the middle of the night to see Jill *(his future wife)*. But he came back — it rained or something.

Ant was very dedicated to the group; it was very much his life. I suddenly got into a social life having discovered girls, basically — and freedom. It was just too good to be true.

I got a car — a battered old Ford Anglia which meant a new-found independence and I went totally over the top.

In my heart of hearts, I was into the band as much as ever, but there was a lot happening to me, apart from the group at that time.

When I talk to friends about certain stages of their life — like what they were going through at about that time — their lives were so much more fun. Saturdays were days off, they'd watch the sport, they'd get out of their heads and relax.

Life for us was exciting and satisfying, but I wouldn't say it was fun. We were achieving something, we were getting somewhere and we were creating something, but as individuals we were going through a difficult period.

I often think that we missed out on a certain era. After leaving school or university most people learn to relax, but we never really could.

I'm not complaining, because we benefitted in other ways, but it meant that we became rather insular as individuals. There was very little sympathy from one of us to the other if one had a problem. I'm sure that I was as bad an offender as anyone else.

The group could be quite ruthless — it had to be because there just weren't the breaks in those days. There were so few chances to get things going.

I look upon the early stages of the band as two distinct eras. There was our first album, 'From Genesis To Revelation', which we

COURTESY CHARISMA

Between guitarists, 1970.

recorded in our summer holidays. By then, I was a student at Farnborough Tech. We just went into the studio and did it — I could hardly play bass at that time. The next album 'Trespass' was a big change because we really started writing as a group. We became a band; we did gigs.

It was the beginning of the next, and probably the most important, stage.

■ **Three years after forming, Genesis got down to live dates upon which they brought all their inexperience to bear. They were sustained by 'outrageous arrogance', loans, hampers, thrifty cooking and 'The Knife' — a new song which roused audiences in a way their pastoral, acoustic songs had failed to.**

● PETER: I'd been trying to hustle gigs and the first one was a party given by some people called the Barnes, who lived opposite the drive to my parents house. It was a huge disappointment.

We were sure people would be struck by our genius. All they wanted were hits to dance to, but we didn't really know any numbers you could dance to! I think we just had to fall back on some blues numbers and a couple of Stones songs.

● ANT: The first proper gig was at Brunel University. I always remember it because I'd restrung my guitar just before the gig. We did this song called 'In The Beginning' in which the first break was just guitar. Suddenly everything slipped; I'd gone wildly out of tune.

I remember playing, and everyone looking round: there was this terrible wall of sound. I kept turning all the knobs of my guitar the wrong way. It was a nightmare. However, the audience seemed to like it.

● MIKE: For a band who'd never done anything, there was a certain amount of interest. We'd been rehearsing in the cottage for six months so it felt really weird to be playing a live gig and we had no idea how to set up. We'd been used to playing in a circle.

There were great arguments when we got there and Pete was as stubborn as ever. I remember that eventually we ended up in sort of two rows. There was Pete, and someone behind him, and then someone next to him and someone behind him. We were sort of two and two with the drummer in an equally weird position.

We had constant feedback. Having played at the cottage quite quietly, allowing for the odd crescendo, we played flat out all evening and totally deafened ourselves. Anyway we got an encore, which was quite amazing. I can't think why; they were probably all drunk.

● TONY: All I remember about the first gig was that I'd worked out all three settings on my amplifier and then when I finally got there, I just switched the amp up full, put my foot down hard and assaulted my way through the whole evening. I just couldn't believe how different it was to be playing live. We set up in a very strange manner too. We had the PA speakers behind us, and the whole arrangement was very peculiar. We must have looked very odd. We had no idea what to do.

● MIKE: We had the ropiest gear you have ever seen in your life — unbelievable stuff. If you can learn to play with terrible gear without any power, without any volume, it means that when you get hold of some good stuff, you will use it well.

We'd go and play gigs, and there'd be these groups, who would be just as bad as us, probably worse, with the most incredible gear. In the old days it used to be a question of how much equipment was stacked up, you know; the higher it was, the better you were.

Well, our gear never got over the first layer — we were definitely a one-storey group.

● TONY: When we used to leave the cottage for a gig, Richard would pack a hamper. Cold sausages were the main thing, I seem to remember. Other groups used to find this hilarious.

We used to turn up with our little hamper. But in fact, it worked very well. In those days there was no question of special gig food; it was too expensive to eat out and so we brought it with us. It was a very nice way of doing it too.

● MIKE: We were incredibly broke at that stage. Ant's parents and my parents — who accepted that I had to try this thing — used to give us a bit of money each week as well as some vegetables and stuff.

A friend's granny gave us £50, which was a fortune in those days. We put it in the bank.

Richard, our roadie-cum-handy, couldn't drive — which was a big help! His father was involved with Hovis, the bakery, and he gave us an old bread van which we converted. I took Richard out to teach him to drive.

We couldn't do more than forty, and on our first lesson out, he said, "Let me have a go." And I said "No. I'll drive through Dorking." He said, "No, I can do it." So he took hold of the wheel and we made our way towards Dorking High Street. There was a parked estate car — bang! — we smashed straight into it.

The bill came to virtually dead on £50. The guy didn't know we only had £50, but that's what it came to. Richard was unpopular for a few days — and our little stash had gone.

Richard was a very thrifty cook. He used to make these meals which seemed to only consist of potatoes and cabbage — and then you'd grovel underneath the cabbage to find out if there was a main bit and there'd be, perhaps, a little kipper hiding.

Later on during our stay at the cottage, when people used to come down to visit, such as our agent or some prospective big guy from

COURTESY CHARISMA

□ *Steve joins, 1971.*

the city; we'd have lunch. We'd have chicken and then all have to sit there watching the guest tuck into these immense chicken portions, and we'd be left with the scraps. It never got us anywhere actually, giving those people the large portions.

All these stories used to get back to us about keeping a picnic hamper in the dressing room. The fact was that we couldn't afford to eat, so we'd get some cold sausages, baked potatoes and boiled eggs and that was our meal for the day at the gig.

You could feed about five people for about £1 in those days, or 50p if you had sausages and baked potatoes. So it really wasn't the height of luxury.

● PETER: Tony and I used to go up to the Marquee to see the Nice, who, unlike ELP, were very concise and, I'd say, unpretentious as well as extremely powerful.

Around that period, there was Hendrix, Vanilla Fudge, the Nice, but not too many others that were both musical and powerful. I remember sitting down at the piano trying to write something that had the excitement of 'Rondo' by the Nice.

I played the first riff to Tony, and he was obviously into it because they were a band that we both liked. After that, Tony did the second section and then we pieced 'The Knife' together.

● TONY: We realised that after we'd played 'The Knife', everyone applauded very loudly and got on their feet and so we decided to play this at the end of our set to get an encore. It was the old trick. The audience did really seem to like it. We weren't so sure. I mean, it wasn't our favourite and it certainly wasn't my favourite track off 'Trespass'. I think we almost went off it because it seemed to be so popular with the audience. That's how perverse we were in our thinking you know.

I think it was the rhythm of 'The Knife' that went down so well. It was the heyday of the idiot dancer — heads going up and down.

I think we appealed to people who liked things to be a little bit more eccentric. For a start, our gear looked as if it had been thrown together. It was cheap and there was an odd selection of instruments. Mike used to play a cello on one number and we also used to have these 12-string guitars which were pretty much unknown at that point. Then, of course, Pete used to play the flute and bang on a bass drum.

● PETER: The bass drum was something that allowed me to participate in the loud sections of the music. I'd feel left out whenever a song would build up to a tremendous climax, as I didn't have a guitar to wave around and Tony was incredibly possessive with the keyboards. All I was left with was my tatty history as a shaky drummer which led me onto the bass drum.

● TONY: Peter played very loud and he was often extremely out of time. I used to have to say "Shut that thing up" because it was putting me off.

● PETER: I felt we needed to get some balls into our act because I knew that we weren't cutting it. I remembered from our earlier flirtations with blues music that we'd had a certain amount of aggression which we now lacked. We changed our act so that we'd come on, as we'd always done, as polite, middle class wimps playing melodic, inoffensive acoustic music, and then, by the end of the act, we'd launch into 'The Knife' and I'd be smashing things up and throwing cymbals around. It was as aggressive as we could get.

We could win over virtually all the small audiences, and it was interesting to see at which point in the act they would actually be won over. It meant we were able to play the acoustic stuff with confidence, even though we had not yet played the electric.

I used to try and wear odd stage clothes. I knew no-one else was into performing, and I would sometimes feel ashamed of the way they looked. At the same time, I knew that I wasn't going to change them, so the only thing for it was to make sure that my own performance was very powerful.

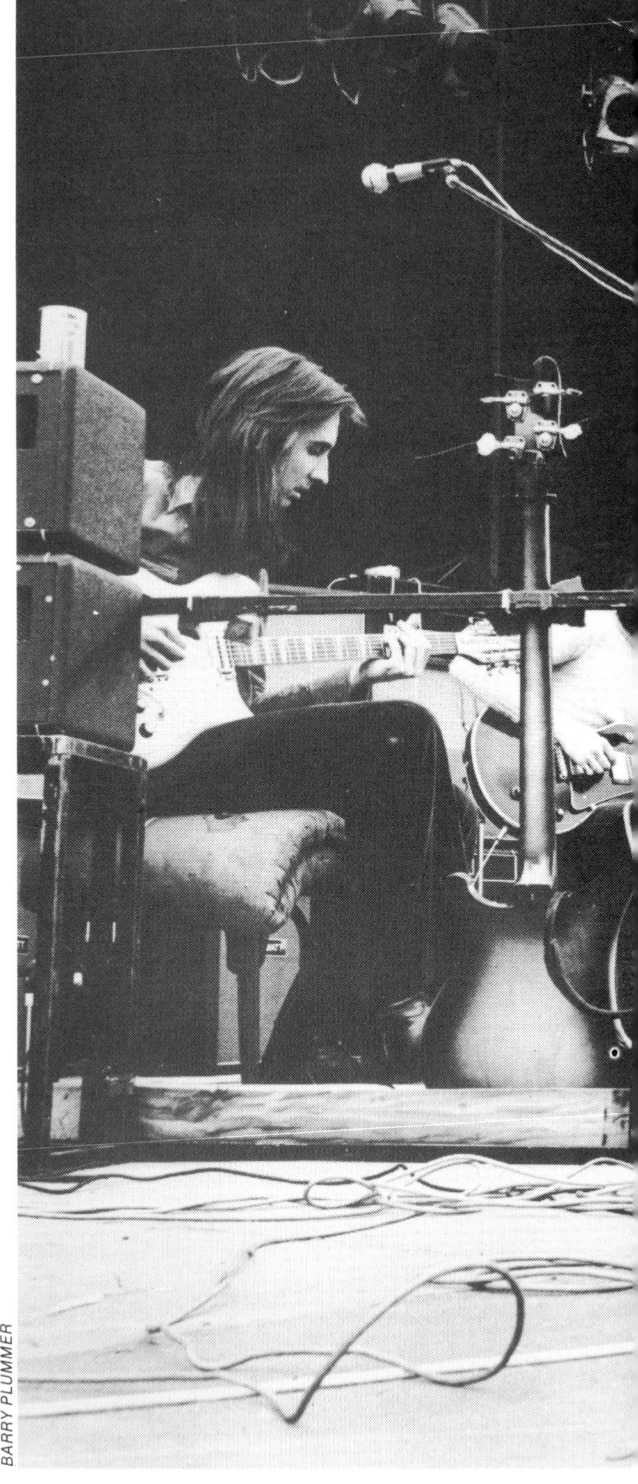
BARRY PLUMMER

□ *Lincoln Festival, 1971.*

I felt that we were failing because everyone in the group would be sitting down and not giving a shit about the audience. It was a very inward looking attitude — that if the audience weren't able to appreciate us, they were dumb. Really arrogant!

I think Chris Briggs, who is now A and R at Phonogram, once promoted a concert with us

at Leicester University and referred to us as, 'snotty-nosed bastards' — although he later denied it.

At the time, we were outraged and very hurt because he'd seemed friendly to us. But now, looking back, I can quite understand. At that time, I felt I had the difficult job, of trying to be the acceptable, human face of Genesis.

I think there were times in the early years when a certain amount of outrageous arrogance was the only thing that allowed us to continue.

I think Ant and Tony were probably the worst offenders in some ways. They were blind to how people were really reacting to the music, which wasn't very well!

■ In March 1970 Charisma boss Tony Stratton-Smith saw Genesis at Ronnie

Scott's Club and signed them up. That summer they recorded their first 'real' album.

●ANT: In many ways Peter was probably more realistic than the rest of us; he was more aware of the realities of turning our music into a saleable proposition. I think this partly explains the visual stuff which he adopted later, as this really helped to take the group from being a sort of minority cult group into something much bigger.

●PETER: Throughout the group's career, I think, I was the one doing the hustling and trying to link them up to the real world.

It was always a sort of gamble, and my grandfather on my mother's side was a considerable gambler. I've always liked the feeling that there is a risk element — that something around me may go well or badly.

The trouble with hustling was that I wasn't very good at it. I would go in, as I see many people do today, and get palmed off by the telephonist, or receptionist. You end up spending the whole day there, and you don't get to see anyone.

Occasionally, one of the others would come with me to give me moral support, but they usually had better things to do. They didn't seem to take it that seriously. I thought this was dumb because, if we didn't get a deal, nothing was going to happen. They used to think that they could just go on making music in the cottage.

However, I remember quite clearly the time I approached Warner Brothers. I found out the christian name of the Managing Director and walked right in and said, "Is Ian back from lunch?" The receptionist said, "No." To which I replied, "OK, I'll just go and wait in his office then." She was nervous because it sounded like I was a personal friend of the MD.

This way I got right into the inner sanctum, and was able to hand over the sweaty little tape. Not that it did any good but at least the rejection came from the top.

I remember Tony and I going to see one agency, and the guy sat us down in his office. He listened to the music and then, very deliberately, told us that we should go back to whatever we'd been doing before, giving us some good reasons why.

I felt as if a black cloud which had been hovering in the distance had actually come down and engulfed us. It was most unpleasant. The worst of it was that we'd go straight back to the rehearsal room to play this music — this magic that we were convinced could inspire the world!

The dangerous thing when you become divorced from reality is that you think that you're God's gift to this, that or the other, and you don't pay attention to the reasons why you're not presenting the stuff properly — why it's not projecting and why you're not getting through.

There was a guy called Marcus Bicknell who at one point looked as if he was going to manage us. He was enthusiastic, but he didn't have any money or influential contacts. In the end, we decided to stick with him until we could find a more powerful manager.

JILL FURMANOVSKY

'The Musical Box'.

It wasn't as callous as that, because when we first talked to him, we intended to go along with him, but, at the same time, there was also a rich garage owner who talked about investing money in us, which we needed to buy basic equipment and a PA, and this was the be-all and end-all of the band's desires at that point.

There was another guy called Alec, who did a tape with us at Ant's house. This tape then got into the hands of Paul Samwell-Smith, who was then producing Cat Stevens and was the hot producer of the time.

He agreed to go into the BBC studios with us at Shepherd's Bush, and do a demo of some music which was going to be for a TV programe. I think it was for an *Arena* programme about a painter, a classic futuristic film of the thirties called *Alphaville*.

Paul Samwell-Smith did the demos with us, and that was the first time that I ever thought Genesis sounded good. The others were very suspicious of Samwell-Smith because of surrendering power to someone else. I was cer-

Tony, 1973.

tain that he was making us sound better than we could do on our own.

● MIKE: We were playing at Ronnie Scott's. We had a residency there to which normally six to eight people would come, about four of whom were our friends. Strat *(Tony Stratton-Smith, boss of the Charisma label)* came one night, and seemed to like us.

We'd played a lot of gigs by then and were getting slightly more polished. Pete had developed a sort of stage personality, swaying around to his bass drum. Some of the material was too complex in the terms of the writing; there was a lot of stopping and starting, but we must have sounded quite professional by then.

Strat got excited, and we signed to Charisma fairly soon afterwards.

It was a nice label, full of new bands — Van Der Graaf Generator, us, Lindisfarne, the Nice, who were still very much around and regarded as the 'biggies'. We were on £10 a week each for the first year, I think. But the main thing was that they supported us — suddenly we became their problem.

● TONY: After we'd signed to Charisma, we started recording 'Trespass' and it was definitely a lot better than the previous album. We still had no idea of recording techniques and for 'Stagnation' Mike and Ant recorded the guitar parts three or four different times, the original idea being to choose between them.

In the end we mixed all the guitar parts onto one track, which meant we got a very blurry sound, which was quite pleasing, although it wasn't what we intended at all.

● PETER: The lyrics for 'The Knife' were partly me being a public schoolboy rebelling against my background. I'd been heavily influenced by a book on Gandhi at school, and I think that was part of the reason I became a vegetarian as well as coming to believe in non-violence, as a form of protest. And I wanted to try and show how all violent revolutions inevitably end up with a dictator figure in power.

Ant and I used to enjoy playing with the words. We would write poems which had nothing to do with songs. He was into flowery, romantic visions, whereas I was into the darker and altogether more mysterious side of life.

When I look back, it really makes me cringe, but I guess it was all part of growing up.

I think 'Stagnation' is one of the numbers

RON DUGGINS

□'*Watcher Of The Skies', Sheffield City Hall, 1973.*

which I still regard as archetypal early Genesis. It was one of our more original numbers.

■**After their first 'real' album came their first 'real' crisis in July 1970 when Ant bowed out.**

●ANT: We'd been on the road for about three or four months when I decided to quit. This has often been presented as 'musical differences' and, although there was some truth in this, the main reason was that I started getting incredible stage fright. That's the truth.

It was one of those things where, if I'd really been able to talk to the others about it, it probably would have been OK, but, as it was, we all found it difficult to communicate properly.

Initially, I had butterflies like everybody else. The fact that we weren't sleeping much and getting no exercise meant that a lot of tension built up within the group.

I was seventeen at the time and had never confronted anything like this before in my life. I absolutely dreaded going out on stage.

This went on for a while, and, as I said, it should have been really easy to talk about and laugh off — but that doesn't take into account our public school background!

I think I probably realised during 'Trespass' that I was going to have to leave.

I desperately wanted to make a very good album and I hoped that things would get better.

During that period, my feelings about the group became very clouded. I still loved the idea of it, but my health was terrible. There were one or two other aspects in the group which weren't absolutely right as well and I think that even if I hadn't fallen ill, somebody would have had to budge sooner or later.

I might have stayed for a while, I don't know. But in the end I had no choice. I was just exceedingly unwell and very disenchanted.

●MIKE: I had long conversations with Ant about his stage paranoia. However, there wasn't much I could do because you can't help someone if they're on stage, even if you're standing next to them.

You can smile and try and cheer them up, but it was something that was going on deep inside him — a sort of sheer terror. As a result, Ant was losing interest and he was very disillusioned.

I also think that out of all of us, Ant found it the hardest to compromise. In a group there's always a certain degree of compromise and with four strong writers there had to be a lot of compromising. But, Ant was, I'd say, the strongest influence at the time — the key member, I think, if there was a key member. This meant there could be no alternative. He was either with us, or he wasn't. He could either take it, or he couldn't. Nowadays, it is very different. Phil Collins' marriage broke up *(in 1979)*, and we took nine months away from

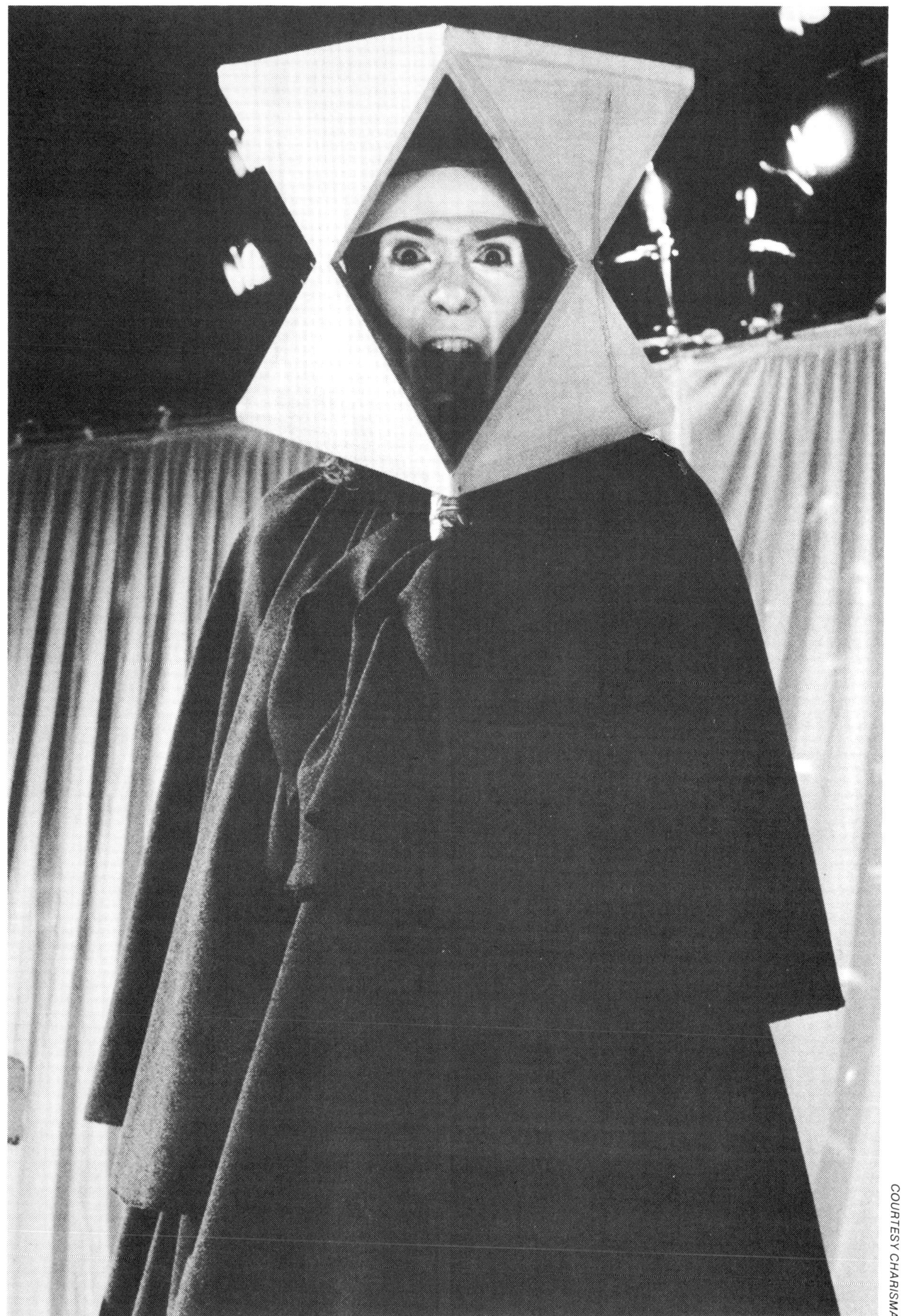

COURTESY CHARISMA

□ *Peter, 1973.*

□ *Phil, 1973.*

the band to try and help him get over it.

Nowadays, our personal lives matter and we make allowances for them — which wasn't the case then.

● ANT: After I had left, I really didn't know too much about what Genesis was up to. I didn't deliberately turn radios off. I even went to a few gigs afterwards, and I thought they were tremendous.

I remember seeing them at Godalming Blues Club doing 'Musical Box.' I thought it was marvellous. But then I started studying classical music, and I became involved with a whole different musical world.

It's been difficult in some ways, because if Genesis had not been so successful, then I would never have had cause for regret. Obviously the fact that they have done so well has meant that I would be completely dishonest if I said I'd never had any regrets. However, if I sit and think about it logically, I realise I could not have stayed and worked within that environment for very much longer.

● TONY: I think up until that point, Ant had been the most important member, and so when he left I thought there was no way of carrying on.

I'd watched Ant getting more and more ill at ease about going on stage. It was very obvious that he wasn't happy doing it. At the time I thought it was all a little bit childish, and he'd probably get over it — no trouble.

I thought there was something magical about the four of us being together — the original four and that when one of us left, that would be it.

● MIKE: Later on Ant and I discussed it in detail and, to be honest, I really couldn't see any solution. The group either stopped for a year and waited for Ant to get himself together and get healthier, or we carried on without him, which seemed to be out of the question at the time. I never considered it, neither did Pete nor Tony. I remember we played our last gig in Haywards Heath — to about 25 people — and that was it.

Afterwards, I drove back from the gig with Pete; just the two of us. We discussed it and said, "Well, that's it." And then, somehow we got round to discussing how we could carry on.

I remember the whole conversation very vividly, actually. Pete was driving this Hillman Imp which used to be the group car and when he started talking he'd be all over the road. I'm digressing here, but it's a part of our life. We were going along in third without realising it, talking away, and suddenly we tuned into the car, which was making a terrible noise. The poor old car was eventually scrapped, mainly because Pete drove to most of those early gigs in third.

Anyway, we suddenly got into this conversation about, "Is this the end?" and by the time we'd got to his parents' house in Woking, we'd decided that there was no real reason to stop.

The two of us decided that we were definitely going to carry on whatever, and then Tony who'd originally believed it to be the end as well, also decided to stay.

Ant leaving was the only time I really thought, "That's definitely it." No doubt about it — I really thought that gig was our last!

After we decided to carry on we discussed the next stage and it was agreed we should not only find a replacement for Ant but also look for a new drummer. John often got overlooked and, although he worked so hard and so well, he was a slow learner and didn't produce many ideas.

So John was told, which is always a difficult experience, but I don't think he was that surprised, actually.

COURTESY CHARISMA

□ *Steve, 1973.*

COURTESY CHARISMA

□ *Mike, 1973.*

JILL FURMANOVSKY

JILL FURMANOVSKY

JILL FURMANOVSKY

JILL FURMANOVSKY

□Seen sharing a joke with the author, Dundee, 1980.

ANDY HANSON

□ *Wembley, 1981.*

R ELLIS

□ *Milton Keynes, 1982.*

JILL FURMANOVSKY

EX115BK2

REX FEATURES

3

1970-1973

Phil Collins was born in January 1951 in Chiswick and was educated at Chiswick Grammar School and the Barbara Speake Stage School; he was a child star of knitting patterns, Smiths Crisps promotions, 'Calamity The Cow' and 'Oliver', as well as being drummer with Flaming Youth, and was introduced to the band in September 1970 via Charisma chief Tony Stratton-Smith.

● PHIL: My mum's a children's theatrical agent and my father was in insurance for forty years. My brother is now a cartoonist — a very successful cartoonist. My sister was an ice-skater for a long time, and now she's involved in the production side of the West End.

I remember my uncle giving me a drum, which I just kept hitting. About three weeks after getting a new toy, kids usually start losing interest. Apparently though, I kept bashing away on it, and so, when I was five, my uncle made a set of drums for me. It was built up on a criss-cross base with triangles, tambourines, cymbals and little toy drums attached by poles. It all fitted into a suitcase.

I remember sitting in the front room playing along to the television, and I have very vivid

JILL FURMANOVSKY

□ *'More Fool Me', 1974.*

MICHAEL PUTLAND/LFI

1973.

memories of playing along to *Sunday Night At The London Palladium*.

I had that kit until I was about twelve, I think. Then my mum bought me a proper drum kit, which I kept until about ten years ago.

If I hadn't been a drummer, I know I'd have been a footballer. I always wanted to be a footballer, but I stuck with the drums.

The drummer had a sort of respectable role within a group. Singers were always quite the opposite — they wiggled their bums and things like that, which didn't appeal to me at all.

I used to play in front of the mirror to the Shadows' 'Dance On' and Joe Brown's 'Only Took A Minute'.

As I got a bit older I must have started buying *Melody Maker* and stuff like that. I always remember that I wanted to be in their gossip column, The Raver. I used to cut out bits about groups — in fact I recently unearthed a whole bunch of scrap-books, which was very embarrassing.

I used to come back from the Marquee and I actually used to write reviews of the gigs and other stuff.

I got involved in acting through my mother, who was starting up an agency. At that time she worked from home and I would be sent off to model knitting patterns and do the voice-overs for TV ads and things like that. Eventually I got sent to audition for the Artful Dodger in *Oliver*.

I was at grammar school at this point, and the headmaster said I could only work for three months out of the potential nine month run, so I left and joined the stage school although I actually ended up doing only seven months of it because my voice broke and I couldn't sing all the notes.

I used to get through about four or five packets of Tunes every night before I went on. I was paranoid about my throat. I still am actually.

I liked playing the Artful Dodger. It was easy for me to do, but knitting patterns and things like that.... The worst job I ever did was in a children's film called *Calamity The Cow*, in which I played the eldest of four kids in a family. The idea was that we had a cow, which was going to win the county show. Anyway, the cow got stolen and we found it just in time to enter it for the competition.

I was sixteen at the time, and I didn't get on with the director at all. I had ideas about the way I wanted to play the part and how I should deliver certain lines, but he wanted me to play it down and act as if I were about eleven or twelve. We used to have lots of small arguments, which I remember as being quite fraught, but I guess it couldn't have been that bad. Anyway, he wrote me out of the script. I went on holiday half-way through the film and came back just in time to help the cow win the county show!

Occasionally, I would get sent to dancing auditions, which I hated. I passed one, it was for a promotional tour for Smiths Crisps which did the rounds of all the Locarnos and Mecca places.

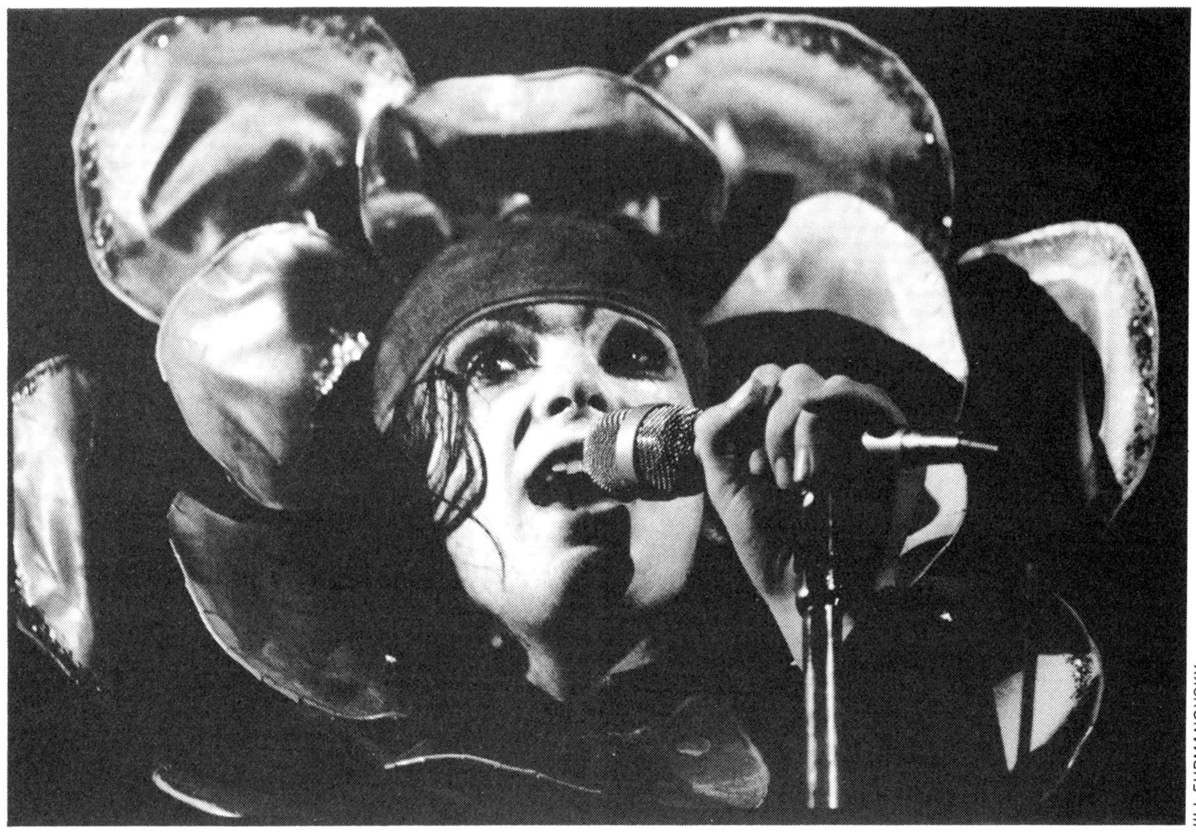

JILL FURMANOVSKY

'Supper's Ready', 1973.

There were four of us — two blokes and two girls. We'd go out on to the floor and dance and the place would be packed with skinheads. I had this completely white outfit — white T-shirt, white trousers, patent boots — and I had to go out and dance in front of all these skinheads. I'd have much preferred playing to them.

Of course we got heckled and stuff, specially when we had to demonstrate the dance to encourage people on to the floor. It was horrible. God, I hated it.

My first group was the Real Thing. We all took it very seriously and used to rehearse almost every day after school. I used to sing and drum at the same time then, because no-one else could sing. Andy, who later became my wife, used to be one of the back-up singers.

We used to model ourselves on the Who and on the Action and do a lot of Motown stuff. It was a good group.

The Gladiators were basically a four-piece soul group and they wanted musicians to back them. Hickory was the band that were formed to back them and I was brought in on drums.

Then, we started getting better than the Gladiators, so we split from them, and changed our name to Flaming Youth.

Ken Howard and Alan Blaikely, who managed Flaming Youth, gave us some songs which we recorded on an album in about two weeks. It was very schizophrenic because we used to go to gigs and play our regular band stuff at the beginning of the set and then follow that with the album material. People who'd liked the first part generally hated the second.

We had a burst of publicity with Flaming Youth when our album, 'Ark 2', came out. That was about it — a blaze of publicity and very little work. After a year, I decided that it was going nowhere and I left. I then started to audition for various bands.

One of the auditions was for Genesis. I read an ad which said: "Tony Stratton-Smith requires a drummer sensitive to acoustic music and twelve-string guitarists."

I remember going to the Marquee one night and chatting up Strat at the bar and saying "Listen, about this group, which group is it?", and he said "Oh, it's Genesis." I'd noticed their name a lot in the back pages of *Melody Maker*, they seemed to play a lot of gigs. I thought I was onto something and that Strat might even give me the job because I knew him. But I had to do the audition.

At the time, I was a huge fan of certain groups. The Action were one of my favourites; in fact, they still are. I had fantasies about being in that group, and also about being in Yes.

This was before I joined Genesis and I used to go and see Yes every week at the Marquee. I happened to be next to a bloke in the audience, who told me that they were looking for a new drummer as Bill Bruford was leaving to go to university. So I went backstage and introduced myself to Jon Anderson. He said "Well, great man, great. Give us a ring on Tuesday and come down for an audition."

I never rang. I never went. I've always wondered about that, because I knew the songs backwards. I'm sure I'd have got the job and would have ended up in Yes.

Genesis were auditioning on the patio outside Peter's parents' house. Mike came up to me wearing a dressing-gown and slippers. He'd actually driven from somewhere in his dressing-gown and slippers. I thought, "God, this is incredible."

There was a swimming pool in the back garden, and they said "Go and have a swim while you're waiting because there are three or four other blokes to be auditioned first." I just couldn't believe it.

I knew all the parts they were being auditioned on; they were asking everybody to play bits of 'The Knife', and bits of 'Stagnation' — a mixture of gentle and heavy stuff. I knew it backwards by the time it came round to my turn.

Peter had said to the bloke before me, "Do you want to warm up?" He replied, "Yeah, I wouldn't mind 10 minutes." I watched as he did this flashy drum solo for ten minutes warming up, and I thought, "No, no — that's not the way to do it. I'm not going to do that."

When it came to my turn, they asked me if I wanted to warm up. I said "No, it's OK, I want to cruise straight in." Tony started to play something, and said "Just play along."

And that's what I did. Not only did I know it backwards, but I was pretty quick having got used to playing different types of music in various different bands. I think I must have made it look very easy.

Peter is what you might call rather vague. He has always been like that and that's how he was when he told me that I'd got the job. He just rang up and said "Um, ah, well, we'd, er, like, um, well, if you'd like to come down and sort of play with us and um..."

That's how he is — positive, but vague.

● MIKE: Phil was just so quick and so natural. He made things sound good straight away. Up until then, it had always been the four of us playing, with the drums as a rather separate entity.

Ever since Phil joined, the drums have been very important, they added another dimension automatically, which drums can do if they're played well and right.

Drummers are often the funniest guys in the band — and Phil very definitely was a new source of energy and humour.

● PHIL: I think a drummer is like the goal-keeper of groups; the person that the others tend to fall back on. I was definitely classed as the clown — which, I think, helped to break the ice.

● PETER: There was a definite change when Phil came into the band. He was a real drummer — something I was never that convinced of with Chris Stewart or John Mayhew. Up until then, we were a group of fairly ramshackle musicians, trying hard to communicate through our music. Most of our ideas were in the form of songs and riffs and melodies — playing our instruments was somewhat secondary.

Phil was not really a writer at that point, but a musician, and a very good and professional one. He changed our attitudes and brought us closer together as a band.

Phil actually knew musicians, which was something that the rest of us didn't. We'd come across a few on the road and got friendly with some that we toured with, but were never part of a circuit of musicians who went to clubs and did sessions.

I remember the first phone call I had with Phil — he told me that he'd played on a George Harrison session, which impressed me a lot. He was actually second tambourine, I think, but he had played alongside one of the Beatles — that was big time!

Phil was always very approachable, he also knew a lot of people. He could actually touch people; he would put his arm around someone's shoulder when he was talking. This is something I can do nowadays, but, at that time, it was a big problem. I was more of a neurotic, middle-class, English, socialising-at-a-distance type person.

● PHIL: There were incredible arguments after I joined. I didn't understand these internal frictions — I didn't know Tony that well, he seemed like a very nervy bloke. Someone would say something, and he'd just storm off.

He would just go off for a walk, and I'd be sitting there twiddling with my drumsticks until he came back. I didn't really know what the hell was going on. I was used to bands that were 'all mates', and, if you wanted to say something, you came out and said it, or you hit somebody or whatever. This seemed like a very tense situation.

● MIKE: We did a few months as a four-piece after Phil joined. It was hard for Tony and I, but at the same time it was quite a good period, I think. We got on a bit better. Tony was under a strain, I think, having to play a lot of Ant's stuff as well. The odd cup of tea went over people — over Margaret actually, his wife. I'd always worked with another guitarist, so suddenly I found I had to work much harder. And, of course, my playing improved. It was difficult playing some of the old songs with just myself and Tony playing the instruments. But, by the time we mastered them and just before we got the next guitarist, Mick Barnard, we wrote 'Musical Box'; we had actually worked as a four piece. It showed how we could adapt.

● TONY: It was quite frightening at times playing as a four-piece. It was probably then that I advanced most as a musician as I was required to play two parts together on stage.

By the end of that period, we were starting to come together. The final thing we wrote as a four-piece was 'The Musical Box', which was pretty much as it ended up on 'Nursery Cryme', minus the guitar part.

■'Trespass' was released by Charisma in October 1970 and after a short four-piece stint, the band played for a few months with Mick Barnard, a guitarist from Aylesbury — one of the first areas where Genesis built up a strong local following.

●MIKE: Mick just didn't feel quite right somehow. But he was good and he was getting better all the time. He stayed with us for about six months on the road.

I think I was partly to blame for looking for the ultimate guitarist to replace Ant. There was just no such thing. We needed to find someone with something different. We were in touch with about 80 guys, believe it or not, and I was actually ill in bed at the time.

The others saw an advert in *Melody Maker*, which Steve had put in, and they got in touch.

They came down with Steve to see me — he was dressed in black, totally in black. That was his initial image. He was great. He was into very strange guitar sounds, and what's more, he liked acoustic guitar, especially 12-string. He had a feel for it which was obvious as soon as he started to play in my bedroom.

■Steve Hackett was born in February 1950 in London. He was brought up in Pimlico and attended Sloane Grammar School. His regular advertisement in Melody Maker's small ads section, seeking 'receptive musicians determined to strive beyond existing stagnant music forms', was spotted by Peter at the end of 1970.

●STEVE: I was born in London. I grew up for the first three years of my life around Brixton, Clapham and Stockwell. After that we moved to a huge council estate in Pimlico.

I grew up, really, in a succession of council flats, with one exception. We emigrated, as a family, to Canada when I was seven years old. My parents didn't like it and we came back after only four months.

My father worked for Shell in the sales department. He started selling his paintings on Bayswater Road and he found that the money he was getting was more than he was making at Shell.

I just managed to get into a grammar school. I wasn't a particularly academic type. I was better at languages than anything else. I wasn't any good at maths.

I didn't receive any musical education at school. In fact, I took up the guitar as a kind of alternative to my school educaton. It was something that allowed me to take on the role of both master and pupil. I like that — it gave me a kind of freedom.

At the age of sixteen, I found that school life conflicted with my social life. It was O levels versus women. It was very difficult because I'd bust up with my girlfriend, and I was still very much in love with her. Not surprisingly, because she let me ravish her.

I went back to school, and I thought, "This is no good." I was sixteen years old, with just enough O levels to scrape through into the sixth form. So, I was studying Racine in French, and suddenly I thought, "Hang on a minute. I want to get out in the outside world. I want to get into a band." At sixteen I wanted to join a band.

It wasn't until I was twenty-one that I managed to earn a living at it. But at sixteen, I split from school. It took about five years of constantly advertising in *Melody Maker* to get into a band.

When I started out playing the guitar I had two separate styles. On one hand I was influenced by all of the blues bands and on the other I had leanings towards classical music. I was thinking, "Groups are great, and they've got the energy, but they don't have the intricacy of some of the Bach fugues and things like that."

I teamed up with a bunch of guys called Quiet World in 1970 and made an album with them. Their attraction, as far as I was concerned, was the fact that, not only were they nice guys, but they had a recording contract. Out of all the five hundred guys that I'd met over that period that had answered the ad, they were the only ones who actually had a recording contract.

We recorded an album but it was an experience in how not to do things, as there were a great many power struggles going on between individuals. For instance, certain members of the band were allowed to be present at the mixes, whereas others weren't.

Meanwhile, my ads in *Melody Maker* were getting longer and longer. I noticed that the ads that stood out were the ones that spent time and money on their little soliloquies. I stuck in this ad saying 'Guitarist/Writer seeks receptive musicians, determined to strive beyond existing stagnant music forms.'

Pete Gabriel phoned me up, and said "I liked the ad. Have you heard of Genesis?" I replied, "Oh, they're like Quintessence, aren't they?" I thought it was all joss sticks and Hari Krishna. I was talking to a photographer friend of mine, and I said, "What do you think? Have you heard of this band called Genesis?" He said, "You've heard of them, haven't you? Join them! Don't be so bloody stupid!"

So I thought, "I'll listen to the album." I went into a record shop and listened to it in a booth with something which sounded like the Temptations blasting out next door. I could barely hear it, but what I could hear sounded very interesting indeed. I couldn't tell if it was guitar or keyboard, and that fired me straight away. The 12-string was something which, luckily enough, I'd been working on myself.

I didn't really feel I did an audition because Pete and Tony came to my house. I played to them, along with my brother. I met them as individuals, played them some stuff, and the interaction started from there, really.

□'The Musical Box'.

□Peter, London Theatre Royal, 1974.

● PHIL: I remember meeting Steve down at Tony's flat in Fulham. I think Peter and Tony had already met him, and it was like — bring Mike and Phil down and let's see what they think. He came round with his speaker and a fuzz box.

He plugged in and came out with all these very Fripp sounds and, as we couldn't have Fripp, it was nice to think we had the next best thing. He was always a very dark character Steve — not only did he always dress in black, but he was also quite mysterious.

● PETER: Tony and I went to this little flat in Ebury Bridge Road that belonged to Steve's parents. He and his brother, John, had this tiny room. They started playing the tape, and there was some slight King Crimson influences. There were also some acoustic things with a slightly Spanish flavour, which were very idiosyncratic.

● PHIL: I remember Steve's first gig, which was at City University — I wasn't drinking very much but I had acquired a taste for Newcastle Brown — having just been on tour with Lindisfarne. I was doing perfect drum fills — three inches to the left of every drum.

It must have been so nerve-racking for Steve — first gig with the band, struggling to remember tunes, and there I was, quietly drunk, falling off my drum kit. I can't play when I'm drunk, but I did try hard that night.

Steve must have wondered what he was letting himself in for — seeing me, whom I'm sure he thought was the group's anchorman, completely legless on the drums. What a debut!

● MIKE: Phil's drum roll was about six inches out everywhere; he was tapping the drum the whole way down. The whole band nearly ground to a halt. Luckily Steve slotted in very easily on the road. He came in quietly, and his guitar playing got better. I didn't know him very well for the first couple of years really, because he was very quiet and reserved, apart from when he'd been on the bottle! Then he was great, incredibly funny actually. People often forget this with Steve.

Soon after Steve joined we started writing 'Nursery Cryme'. We went down to Strat's house in the country at Crowborough. There was a room near the garage which other bands had been to, which he let us use.

It was a very hard album to write, because we had to re-adjust. It was one thing to bring Steve in on the road, playing the songs written with the original four of us — but quite another when it came to filling Ant's role as a songwriter.

● STEVE: When I first joined Genesis I saw it as a compromise of sorts. I didn't think, "Hey, they're incredible! I'm a fan." I was very interested in certain textures and styles that they managed to make their own, yet, I found that when it came to the more dramatic moments, that they didn't quite go far enough.

I never felt that it was quite angry enough, nor did I feel that the perspectives in the band were as broad as they should have been.

JILL FURMANOVSKY

□ *Peter, 1974.*

Their backgrounds were different — even for guys that went to Charterhouse together. Peter was a rather different character to Mike and Tony, for instance.

Mike was always the prime diplomat, a kind of glue really holding the band together.

I was a rather awkward person in the sense that I'd developed along my own lines, and then found it very hard to submerge myself into the group identity. I did realise, however, that they had a lot more experience of songwriting than I had.

When I joined the band, I thought, "Well, Pete's obviously the instigator — he's the man who's always on the telephone; he's the main hustler." At the same time I felt that he often found it difficult to explain himself. We used to have surreal conversations, where neither of us really understood what the other was saying.

I loved what Tony played, I was his number one fan in the band. I found the fact that Tony was very reserved frustrating at times. I felt I wanted to be closer to him as an individual, and yet always seemed to come up against the reserve which I guess his education had built in.

I found that all the guys in the band were often very resistant to showing their feelings.

I suddenly realised that there was a difference between these guys and all the bands that I'd been in before. The difference was that always before we had all been good mates, whereas in this situation we weren't necessarily friends, but we were colleagues. We had a working relationship, and we had to go through a lot which was very exhausting and which often made me feel insecure, and that I wasn't quite up to the job. I felt perhaps I might get replaced because I wasn't coming up with enough material or enough songs.

■ **Having settled their line-up, Genesis were brought in as junior partners on the Charisma package tour early in 1971 with Charisma's other two rising stars, Van der Graaf Generator and Lindisfarne. Ticket prices were pegged at 30p (six bob). The tour was successful but on their own Genesis could only rely on a solid following in London and the commuter belt — Watford, Aylesbury, Guildford and Godalming. They could however, create their own excitement even if the audience wasn't always aware of it.**

● MIKE: There was a very strong feeling towards Strat from the others at Charisma to give us the boot — or rather, just to stop worrying about us: "Let them sort of drift out quietly" seemed to be the way they were thinking.

As a result, Strat made a point of putting more money in and pushing us harder. We were rather slow commercially about this period, although there was magic in the gigs, in terms of the relationship between us and the audience. The first Charisma package tour was fantastic because all three bands were fairly unknown. We were on first. We were always on first, bottom of the list. Lindisfarne were second and then Van der Graaf closed the show.

We did two more tours like that over the years, and it all got difficult after a while because, by the second tour, Lindisfarne were doing rather well, yet Van der Graaf were still last on. Lindisfarne were going down better with the audiences than Van der Graaf.

We were caught in the middle somewhere — and egos started to come to the fore.

● PHIL: We played a gig at Watford Hydrospace — I don't remember what was actually said, but Mike and Tony were at each other's throats in the dressing-room. Mike threw a chair at Tony — no, Tony threw a chair at Mike.

Then we had to go out and do an encore — 'The Knife.' As we went out I seem to remember Mike trying to trip Tony up from behind — trying to catch his leg — on the way to the stage.

Once on stage they were friends again; we played 'The Knife' and it was all forgotten when we came off. The atmosphere just changed. There were a lot of those sort of fights.

I remember Tony flaring up at a club in Edinburgh. People were sitting round at tables and drinking — it was a pretty heavy place. Someone set fire to the table while we were doing an acoustic tune. Tony was trying to play the guitar, and the audience were louder than we were.

Tony played a huge chord in the middle of this acoustic number, threw his guitar onto the floor, swore loudly at the crowd, and stormed across the front of the stage to the dressing-room.

One by one we followed, because we couldn't really play without him. The promoter knocked on the dressing-room door and said, "Listen, you can't just walk off."

Then a couple of fans who really liked us came in and said, "You've really got to come back and play." Meanwhile, the tables were still burning. It was only a little fire — plastic cups melting and stuff.

I think we went back and played about 20 minutes and then called it a day. But those kind of flare-ups were happening all the time. I guess we were frustrated when audiences refused to listen to our acoustic set.

● PETER: We had a fantastic audience at Aylesbury — Friars. It felt like our spiritual home.

I think that was the first time that I got to the end of 'The Knife' and started to smash things around. I got so carried away that I jumped into the middle of the milling audience. I hit someone as I fell and I didn't land properly. I had a horrible sensation of something crunching. When I tried to get up, I couldn't.

There was so much adrenalin pumping round my body that I didn't really feel any pain.

I was lifted back on the stage, and although I couldn't stand up, I carried on singing. I thought I'd just twisted something. At the end of the number, the rest of the band walked off and I was left there. People obviously thought, "Oh, he's hamming it up a bit tonight. The old James Brown fainting routine."

By now the pain was incredible and I had to frantically signal to people in the wings to come and help me off. I'd broken by ankle!

● TONY: The funny thing was that, after we finished the set, Pete said, "I think I've broken my ankle." Mike and I said, "Sure, sure" — we refused to take it seriously. Then I took a good look at it and I thought, "Shit, he probably has."

His leg was completely out of shape, the bones were sort of sticking out of his sock. It was horrible. However, we didn't really have much sympathy at all until someone came along and said it was broken.

It was crazy. I don't know what he was doing. He just suddenly threw himself into the audience. It was a very wild thing to do; he must have got very carried away.

● PHIL: At this stage we didn't actually cost a lot of money. We spent an awful lot on transport. We never owned a van, and so we had to hire Reg King's vans, which always broke down.

We played one gig at Aberystwyth University and we broke down three times on the way there and four times on the way back. We arrived after the gig had finished.

There was a certain van that we rented from Reg King, the letters CLP were in the registration number, that one always used to give us trouble. We'd think, "Oh, thank Christ, it's the white one!", or "Great, it's the orange one! We're all right!" If we got bloomin' CLP you knew you were in for a bad night.

Anyway we broke down three times. We arrived there, and everyone was drinking after the gig. So we thought, "Well, we might as well just go home again now."

We had a drink, went home and broke down four times on the way back Peter was learning the oboe at the time and every time we stopped he would practise in an AA box.

We were all waiting for the breakdown man and trying to get to sleep while he played his oboe in the AA box, with a towel round him to keep warm.

■ **As Peter's ankle mended, the band rehearsed for their third album at Tony Stratton-Smith's house in Crowborough, Sussex. 'Nursery Cryme' was released in November 1971 but, in Britain, didn't sell many more copies than 'Trespass' had.**

● TONY: Phil's favourite band at the time was Yes, and he brought some of their playing ability into the group, which was a new departure for us.

It was just a question of being in the rehearsal room together and experimenting, and when something excited one of us, we'd all

BARRY WENTZELL

□ *Peter, 1974.*

respond by playing along with it. It's the way we have always worked.

It's fair to say, I think, that Steve and Phil felt less able to do this — particularly in the early days — because they were the new boys. The three of us were something of a clique.

Phil's a very easy person and I don't really think he found it too much of a problem. I guess it must have been more difficult for Steve.

● PETER: There was undoubtedly an old boy network. I think as Phil and Steve did not come from public school, they thought that the three of us had it all tied up.

We weren't giving away our territory very easily. We originally saw them as musicians, rather than as writers. We were still expecting to do the bulk of the writing.

Steve began to assert himself before Phil, and insisted on getting some songs through. There were some things that we all liked but there was also quite a lot that we didn't. I think that was partly because Steve was less able to manipulate the rest of us then we were.

● PHIL: We all used to throw ideas together and someone would suggest, "How about suddenly going very loud now, or how about stopping completely?" This method of arrangement appealed to me quite a lot.

'Nursery Cryme' is not one of my favourite albums. It sounds as if everybody's playing with two hands on the keyboard. There's huge chords, as well as two guitars and a really big drum sound. Pete's voice is very thick, and as a result, it sounds as if it is all being squeezed on to this bit of tape.

● TONY: 'Nursery Cryme' was a very difficult album. Everything on 'Trespass' we'd already played live and we therefore had a mass of material to choose from.

But since then, apart from 'The Musical Box' which was very popular live and an obvious choice for inclusion on 'Nursery Cryme', we hadn't written anything new and it was a question of trying to write things in the rehearsal room.

The big addition for me was this mellotron which we brought off King Crimson — a great big thing, which created all these sounds that added instant magic. It was King Crimson's third mellotron.

I went round there to collect it and even their roadie seemed 'big time' to me. I felt really self-conscious playing it. The first thing I used it on was the string sound as I didn't really know what else to do. It sounded good and I had this piece I'd written at Sussex University which became the 'Fountain of Salmacis'.

'Fountain of Salmacis' was definitely something totally new. There was much more of a classical feel to it. I think it was the most successful, interesting track on that album.

● STEVE: We were rehearsing one night about six months after I joined. Tony started playing something on his own, which he said was part of a previous number that they'd done. He incorporated the mellotron into the song and I started putting a harp-like effect on to it, which was a very subtle way of playing guitar, but it actually gave it spark.

The whole thing developed into 'Fountain of Salmacis'. The guitar solo at the end was, I think, a breakthrough at the time. Previously we'd had big chords that sounded very orchestral, which I loved; but suddenly there was a solo over the top of that.

It never went down well in front of an audience. Perhaps it was too classically orientated — certainly it was a far cry from straight rock and roll. But we felt it was the best thing we'd ever done.

MIKE: Personally, I think — and everybody else would probably agree — that 'Nursery Cryme' and 'Selling England' are very uneven albums — there are some very high highs, but some very low lows, too.

● TONY: I think one of the most depressing things about 'Nursery Cryme' was the lack of response from the record company. They didn't really seem to like it that much.

I think looking back on it, it's my least favourite of all our albums. Only 'The Musical Box' and 'Fountain of Salmacis' really stand out for me.

If Britain remained unresponsive, Genesis started achieving success in Europe, notably in Belgium and Italy.

● TONY: I think it was at Pete's wedding, that we first heard that 'Trespass' had got to number one in Belgium — whatever that meant — and we were amazed. We had only done one gig in Belgium — a little club where we set up in phalanx form.

● STEVE: For some reason, we'd become number one in Belgium. We used to go over on the night ferry and arrive the next morning, having not slept, because we couldn't even afford bunks.

All we would have to keep us going would be a few beers in the horrible lounge and some smelly sandwiches. We would literally drive straight to the gig, play, and then drive back to the ferry.

We would arrive back two or three days later, and just collapse. We were so determined, that we were prepared to put up with that kind of nonsense.

● PHIL: Belgium and Italy were the two places that liked us, really — apart from Aylesbury Friars and the home counties. It was really all down to Belgian festivals.

I remember throwing up on the boat on the way over there and limping home exhausted.

One night, I decided to call unannounced on Kid Jensen when he was doing his *Jensen's Dimensions* on Radio Luxembourg. Richard, Pete and I drove from Belgium. Pete, as I said

PHOTOFEATURES INTERNATIONAL

□1975.

before, was always very vague. To the onlooker, it would seem as if he was stoned out of his head, although in fact he was as straight as a die. I remember driving along in the Transit and it was freezing cold with snow piling up on the windscreen.

We arrived at Radio Luxembourg at about one-thirty in the morning. I suppose we thought at the time that it was a good thing to do because our albums were always top of Kid's charts in *Sounds* — and were also in the *Jensen's Dimensions* top 30.

However, when we got there, Kid seemed a bit put out that we hadn't rung two days in advance to say we were coming. Anyway we went to the studio and he did the obligatory two minute interview. Then we piled in the van and drove back to where we'd come from.

PHOTOFEATURES INTERNATIONAL

□ *Rael, 'The Lamb' on tour, 1975.*

● PETER: We were sent to Italy most summers as a means of sustaining the band through from college closure in June, until re-opening in October. Every week's income was critical at that point.

Although a lot of people thought that we had silver spoons in our mouths and that we could run back to mummy and daddy for a comfortable place to stay, we weren't actually getting financed.

We had £750 which was borrowed from family and friends at the beginning, and that was an advantage that we had that some others didn't. However I think that most bands starting off, whatever their backgrounds, were given similar amounts by parents and friends to buy their first pieces of equipment.

We weren't special in that way. There are many accusations against us which I think are fair, but I don't think the silver spoon argument is one of them.

● TONY: In Rome we played in front of 20,000 people. That was quite early in our career, and the fact that that many people should want to come and see us seemed quite incredible.

■ **British interest increased in the spring of 1972 when Peter shaved the top of his head for their appearance at the Lincoln Festival in May. It was the beginning of an increasing attention to visual detail.**

● PETER: As the front man, I was very conscious of how we were going down with our audiences. The others would sit still at the back, so the performance really relied on the way I projected it.

Phil was the critical element in terms of the feel of the music and I was the critical element in terms of style and presentation.

I always really felt that the others only tolerated this new visual direction. They knew they were benefiting from it, but they weren't totally happy about it. Maybe it was just because they felt I was steering our music in a way they didn't want it to be steered.

I remember Paul Conroy at Charisma suggested getting someone to dress up onstage in a red dress and a fox's head, to promote our next record, 'Foxtrot'. I think he really fancied doing it himself. And I thought, "Well, damn it, if we're going to do it, I want to do it! I want to be the centre of attention!"

The first gig that we tried it out was at a boxing ring in Dublin. I remember being very nervous as I walked onto the stage in the middle of a number.

The audience was shocked by the weird-

PHOTOFEATURES INTERNATIONAL

□ *1975.*

ness of a man dressed up in woman's clothing and a fox mask — but I loved it! This performance gave me an unquestionable authority, and I thought, "I must be on to something here."

● PHIL: Pete came on stage half-way through 'Musical Box' in a red dress and a fox's head. It was the only moment in the show that he wore anything like that and it must have seemed a bit strange to the punters. We were amused that he had the gall to go out and do it.

When we played the Rainbow, there was a picture of Pete in his fox's head on the front page of the *Melody Maker* — which doubled our earnings straight away. We went from earning £300 a night to earning £600 a night, which was a lot of money in those days. Suddenly people had something to write about — you can't really write about the crashing cymbals, thudding drums and the swirling keyboards for very long. They needed some new angle, and suddenly Peter had given it them. The Rainbow concert was definitely the beginning of all that.

Our songs and words often had more to them than met the eye. They weren't regular rock and roll lyrics. So when Peter started coming in wearing these masks it was just an extension of the fantasy element.

People could sit back in their seats and watch what was going on. By the time of 'The Lamb', we'd moved toward total theatre.

● MIKE: It's always easier to talk about visual things when discussing concerts, than to talk about the music — the pounding bass and the crashing drums. It also got us a lot of publicity.

I did feel awkward when Pete dressed up in the fox mask and the red dress. The moment when he actually got on stage, I felt a bit unsure. It didn't seem to go with anything.

● TONY: Pete's decision to dress up was nothing to do with us. Suddenly he decided to shave his head and wear strange clothes in order to be more of a focal point on stage.

He rather liked being seen as an eccentric, you know — which meant shaving funny bits of his head, putting on white face paint and accentuating his eyebrows. He used to put on all this makeup and it looked very good I think, particularly under stage lights. It certainly made you remember the group, for, at that time, no-one else was doing it.

We'd say no to certain things that we just didn't feel were appropriate. But a lot of the costume ideas were things that only he knew he could carry off.

You couldn't say to Pete, "Do you reckon that you can suddenly prance around on the stage looking like a sort of over-grown dandelion?" It was up to him to make it work.

■ That summer Genesis started work on 'Foxtrot' which was released in October 1972.

● MIKE: 'Foxtrot' is probably one of my favourite Genesis albums, mainly because of 'Supper's Ready'. We wrote some of it at a doctor's house near Chessington, but most of it was written at Una Billing's School of Dancing in Shepherd's Bush. We were in a rehearsal room downstairs which meant that we could hear the banging of feet all day long.

'Watcher of the Skies' was already written, 'Can-Utility And The Coastliners' was written in the rehearsal room and 'Get 'Em Out by Friday' was pretty much a group effort.

It wasn't until we had recorded the album that we realised that we had something really strong. It marked the beginning of another era, I think, the time when Tony, Phil and I took over on the instrumental sections.

There was an element of luck involved. I mean the writing was good, but as we recorded 'Supper's Ready' it started to dawn on us that this was one of our strongest pieces.

● TONY: 'Supper's Ready' was a combination of a lot of different ideas. 'Willow Farm' was a song that Peter had written that started off with a guitar piece of mine, which we turned into something that sounded a bit like 'Musical Box'. Then I thought it would be good to stop the song suddenly and go straight into 'Willow Farm' because it had a great introduction.

On the 'Apocalypse in 9/8' section, Mike, Phil and I were just jamming and I said to Mike, "If you can keep to just these three notes, E, F sharp and B, it will allow me to play an awful lot more chords on top. And that is how it came together. The original idea was to leave some of the sections as chord sequences and then record some vocal harmony parts on top. I came in one day to find that Peter had put all these vocals on it. At first I thought, "This is really annoying. He's singing over the keyboard," but it didn't really take me very long to realise that it was actually very good.

The vocals added drama, and I felt that, as a result, the song reached an incredible peak. I think 'Supper's Ready' is far and away the best thing we've written — not least because of the combination of ideas.

● PETER: There was one particular incident which gave me the inspiration for 'Supper's Ready'. There was this room at the top of Jill's *(his wife)* parents' house. This room was the coldest part of the house. I always used to get the shivers when I went in there.

It was covered in strong purple and turquoise wallpaper. Everything was bright purple and turquoise. Anyway, we had this strange evening up there which ended with Jill feeling like she'd been possessed. It was extremely frightening. I don't know how to explain it — it was as if she had had a fit, or something.

I experienced a sense of evil at that point — I saw another face in her face. I don't know how much of this was going in inside my head and how much was actually happening, but it was an experience I could not forget and was the starting point for a song about the struggle between good and evil.

At times I really felt that I was being led, for there were a number of odd coincidences. Unlikely facts would suddenly come to light, or names would suddenly lead me to other things. I ended up reading *Revelation* in the Bible. This explains the apocalyptic bit at the end of 'Supper's Ready'. I think it was one of the first times that I felt I got a good performance out of my voice because I felt as if I was really singing from my soul — almost like singing for my life.

● TONY: People always used to ask us what it was all about, although it seems fairly obvious reading the lyrics; perhaps it's just that people couldn't believe that something could be that pretentious.

Yet I think it works. As long as one realises it was written with a certain amount of tongue in cheek. The title was definitely not intended to be taken that seriously.

STEVE: People used to come up afterwards and say, "Yeah, Supper's Ready!." I also used to get a lot of very freaked-out chicks saying, "Steve, I actually saw God at the end." What could you say? You couldn't argue with that. You'd say, "You saw God. Great. I was trying to get the notes right."

● PETER: I made sure there was no-one else around when I recorded my part, because I knew that (a) I couldn't do some of the vocals very well and also I would be rather self-conscious, and (b) I was trying stuff that I knew some of the others wouldn't like. I knew that the keyboard solo was too long for the number. It was detracting. There was a great solo in there, but it needed editing. I thought that the only way that I could keep this number working was to get a vocal in. I worked for a long time to get it right.

When the band came in — and they came in together, thank God, I made sure of that! — and I played them the tape, sure enough, Tony was outraged that I'd gone over his sacred solo. However the rest of the band were really excited by what I'd done and popular vote was always the deciding factor. These were the absurd manipulating tactics which we were all guilty of — but probably me, more than any other!

● PHIL: Peter used to try and get everybody out of the studio when he recorded the vocals.

Tony and Mike were always thrown out. Peter preferred to do it this way as he didn't particularly want an audience when he was singing and because some of the time he didn't know what he was going to sing.

Obviously if you've got people there, they

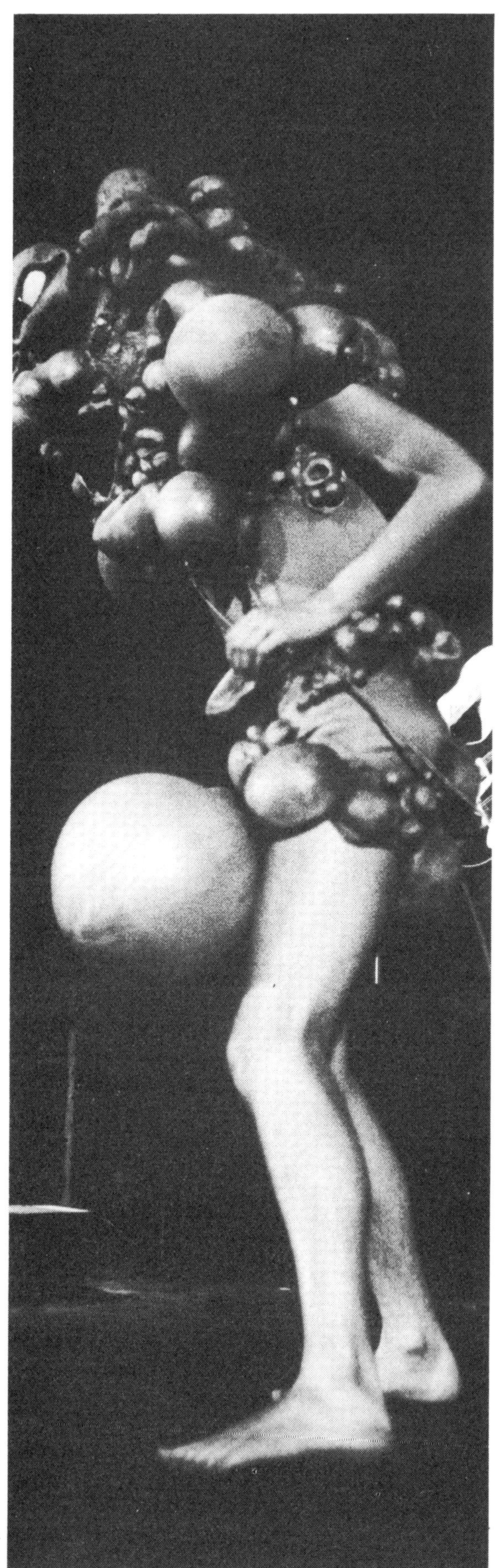

are all going to make suggestions and the whole thing tends to fall apart. I used to stay because I was doing some of the singing with him, and I suppose he thought I wouldn't put a spanner in the works.

Bob Potter was our first producer on 'Foxtrot' and he'd just worked with Dylan and Bob Johnson. However he didn't really like our music and made no bones about it.

A week later, he'd gone. Then we had another bloke, Tony Platt, who was an Island engineer and we didn't get on too well with him either.

John Burns and Dave Hitchcock were the next two; Dave Hitchcock being a Charisma suggestion and John Burns another Island engineer.

John actually really liked the band. He liked us as individuals and was also keen to put a bit of funk into the album.

● PETER: 'Supper's Ready' was a gamble. There was some resistance in the band over the length of it, people were very nervous about it. We were taking risks with stuff that we knew was likely to be uncommercial, which wasn't guaranteed to get radio-play and which was probably going to get knocked in reviews.

TONY: I feel very close to 'Foxtrot' as I had a lot to do with the music on it. 'Watcher Of The Skies' is a good example. There was just something about the first two chords of that song which gave it instant atmosphere. We used it to open the show, this was in the days of the ultra-violet lights and the dry ice — before all that became a cliché — and it didn't matter what you played for the next four numbers, the atmosphere it created could not be destroyed.

● STEVE: I remember at a gig in Italy, Tony started playing the mellotron introduction for 'Watcher Of The Skies'. I was somewhere downstairs in a dressing-room when I heard this sound coming out which shook the foundations of this huge echoey stadium.

It really sounded as if something was coming in to land. I remember thinking that there had been nothing quite like this before in rock music. This epic quality is what Genesis brought to rock music, really.

I know they've been knocked a lot, and I know you can criticize the music for being too pompous, but it did actually have a very dynamic quality to it, combining aspects that had previously been the domain of either the orchestra or the rock band.

● TONY: Mike and I wrote the lines to 'Watcher Of The Skies' in Naples at the back of a hotel, staring out over this landscape. It was totally deserted. It was incredible.

We had the idea of an alien coming down to the planet and seeing this world where ob-

□ *The Slipperman, 'The Lamb' on tour, 1975.*

viously there had once been life and yet there was not one human being to be seen.

●PHIL: Our songs were based on fantasies or mythology or whatever, yet the words to 'Get 'Em Out By Friday' are as relevant today as they were then. I think that this song was the only piece of social comment that we ever did.

●STEVE: On 'Foxtrot', I still had a slight inferiority complex as I felt that I wasn't contributing enough to the band.

I remember saying, "Do you really feel that I ought to leave because I am not writing as much as the rest of you?" Anyway they reassured me by complimenting my guitar playing — which was the first time I really got any feedback from them.

I had an unaccompanied piece on the album called 'Horizons'. It wasn't just a concession to me; it was something that they all liked. I did get more material onto that album than on the previous one, but I was always unhappy with myself as a fledgling song-writer.

I felt that I could do more. I think it wasn't until 'Selling England By The Pound' that I felt that I'd fully developed as an electric guitarist.

●TONY: After we'd finished our previous albums, I thought, "This is not as good as it should be", and yet I was very happy with 'Foxtrot' — I really didn't think there was a weak song on it.

■**'Foxtrot' was the first Genesis album to enter the charts, reaching number 12 soon after release. At the end of 1972 the band made their first foray into America.**

●MIKE: That's Strat for you — a crazy move. He sent us over for a charity show at what is now called the Avery Fischer Hall in New York. It was amazing of him to do that — and it went down a bomb — fantastic.

●PHIL: Tour's too grand a word for it actually. We did two gigs. The first was at the University in Boston, and we arrived there thinking, "OK America. Are you ready for us?" and I'd be surprised if there were thirty people in the audience.

All the students seemed to be carrying lunch-boxes and the books that they were studying. It was an unbelievable setting for a rock concert.

They trickled in, some of them eating, some of them reading.

We played the set, and thought, "This can't be America — not the America we've read about. They're supposed to go wild. They're supposed to like British groups.'

The next night, we went on to New York, and it was a good gig. We had a terrible buzz on the gear. The New York Philharmonic had been rehearsing that afternoon in the hall, for an evening concert the next night, and they wouldn't let us in until six.

Well, the doors opened at seven, and we'd made these grand plans for a three-hour sound check, including a rehearsal of some of the newer material, because we planned to do 'Supper's Ready' and things like that. By half past six, the orchestra had just about got their gear off, but because of the unions we couldn't move our own stuff.

Anyway, we eventually got started and the audience loved it . But Mike came off stage and went straight to the dressing-room and threw his bass on the floor. He was just so disappointed.

I felt it had gone alright but Tony and Mike have always been more affected by setbacks — they want every gig to be perfect.

We had a few drinks, and everyone cooled down a bit — I think we all thought that America had taken to us. That was it; we've played New York, now we're big in America. But 20 miles down the road they hadn't heard of us.

We did a proper tour of the east coast the following year in March, which lasted a month.

●MIKE: We put on a rather bad show, although it was largely due to technical troubles.

I remember coming off stage, thinking that the whole evening had been rubbish. I flung my bass on the floor — what a gesture! — and there was Strat hugging me and saying, "Fantastic!", while I thought it was a pile of crap. It went down very well with the audience though.

We went back to America the following year. We did endless tours for the next six years. America's a big place....

At first we couldn't find anyone whom we could support. We probably could have made it much earlier in America if we'd actually gone out on support — but it was satisfying to feel that when you played somewhere, the audience just came to see you — all 30 of them, you know! Philadelphia was good, Chicago was good; Montreal and Quebec were great.

●TONY: Our record company in America at that stage was pretty useless. They made nothing of 'Foxtrot' at all in the States. I don't actually know whether they could have done or not. The market is different over there.

Even so, as far as they were concerned, it was just another album.

DE PASAPORTES

1973-75

At the beginning of 1973, the band played their first major British tour which secured a large cult following across the country.

● MIKE: We suddenly started to become quite big in England. We were playing all the town halls and suddenly it was goodbye to the clubs.

We are a band who have always put on different sorts of shows — some of which have cost a lot of money, some of which haven't. I firmly believe that it's irrelevant how much you spend; often the best things are the cheapest.

We had this idea of hiding all the gear, having spent the last five years with big stacks of equipment behind us. We just went out and bought a white gauze curtain, which cost us £50, and six ultra-violet tubes and put the curtain in front of the gear.

It worked — it was so simple and easy, yet it gave the stage a very special atmosphere.

● TONY: We had this idea of putting a curtain in front of the gear, transparent to sound, but opaque to sight. The idea was that it would look as though we hadn't any gear on stage apart from the instruments. It was the complete opposite of what some groups were trying to do, which was to have as much gear behind them as possible. I remember playing with one group and discovering that half the cabinets had no speakers in them. We had a total antipathy to that and decided to appear with nothing at all.

By fluke we discovered that when you shone ultra-violet light on to the white curtain, the stage suddenly came alive; the whole curtain became a blue colour, not just where the light fell.

I think it was something to do with the fireproofing of the curtain that caused it to do this. At the same time, Peter came up with these new ideas for costume; he wore a red box on his head for one song and a flower mask. The ultra-violet highlighted these effects in such a way as to make them very dramatic.

It all came together on the first night at the Rainbow in February 1973. It was quite a memorable gig.

● STEVE: All you saw when you looked at the stage was a white muslin backdrop, which didn't look like a backdrop because it was all lit with UV. The whole of the stage glowed at the back.

Peter was a silhouette figure with bat

wings; all you could see were his eyes, which were day-glo.

He did actually look like a being from another planet. It didn't go down too well at a gig in Toronto. This guy started shouting out. Then someone else punched him, and then the whole place was in an uproar. We were supporting Lou Reed at the time. It was an ill-conceived combination!

● PETER: When things were getting too pretty and twee and too English public school I would try and introduce a little weirdness or menace so that there was a darker side. It seemed as though the aggression and weirdness would get us through when we played gigs in more industrial areas, where I felt the prettiness seemed rather out of place. I think the sound of the two 12-string guitars was universally attractive but as a band we were being rejected unless we had that darker edge.

When you get up on stage, you are in an artificial situation — you are not acting normally. Your choice of artifice then becomes the determining factor.

The critical element for me was how much feeling we were able to put out.

There were good and bad gigs, but I think there was always — even though it was often filtered or blocked — a real emotion actually getting through.

Even though we weren't getting through to the press, we were getting through to a very mixed audience. It wasn't just middle class music, which is how it's often portrayed today. We were getting through to different social groups.

There were certain areas such as southern America and certain towns in England, which were only interested in heavy music. But, in places that were open to a few other things, I think we began to get a foothold.

● PHIL: The visual thing started working for us in a way as Pete became the obvious focus of attention. But eventually that started back-firing internally.

I know I felt frustrated, we would play a good or a bad set and people would just ignore it and say, "Yeah, you looked good tonight."

There were a couple of concerts when Peter decided to fly at the end of 'Supper's Ready'. In London, Drury Lane, and New York. He would throw off the black cloak with his red triangle box head to reveal a white made-up face and a white costume. He would then go up into the air suspended from a Peter Pan rope. It worked OK in London, although he nearly got strangled in New York. A bloke pulled up the wire before Peter was ready and he did the song spinning round in circles, with his arm wrapped round his head, and trying to right himself with his leg.

● STEVE: The rest of us were a bit boring — we all just sat there. At the time, I thought that you could make a success out of music which produced images in people's minds, and that there was no need to dress up and leap around.

I sometimes used to find Peter's contribution embarrassing. Eventually I saw that it provided something to look at, rather than the unemployed-singer-syndrome of a guy running around on stage, waving a microphone round in the air and pretending to break it.

● MIKE: There were so many bands around who were playing either rock and roll or heavy metal, and that was it. They were much better than us, so we didn't try to compete. It wasn't an intentional "Let's be different" sort of thing — it just happened naturally.

I spent the first three years of my playing career on a chair, and it took me a while to get up. It's as simple as that. It wasn't as if we were saying, "We're intellectual, moody and tense; we've got to sit down, man!".

It had a lot to do with personalities. I wasn't a great stage performer, and neither was Steve. When it came to writing lyrics, we'd listen to the music, and find that we couldn't write about some of the very grand moments. It just sounded wrong to write about 'on the streets', 'sex and drugs', it wasn't our style.

We had a rather grandiose, epic quality, which suggests a certain kind of lyric. It's rather hard to say "I love you", or "Stay with me tonight", over that sort of music.

● PHIL: Everyone was reading science fiction. I wasn't reading at all, but Tony and Mike and Pete would often swap books and ideas, and quite a lot of the lyrics obviously came from science fiction.

● MIKE: We used to write fantasy lyrics, drawing from Greek mythology and telling little stories and stuff like that. It seemed to go with the music at that time, and it was something we all used to enjoy reading about. And yet, there we were, going down a bomb in Newcastle!

I've got this theory that, in the countryside, they yearn for the town which means that they really like straight rock and roll, but in the cities, they want escapism, which is I think what we provided.

● PHIL: Our fans were mainly college-goers — spotty blokes, most of them. We never had girl fans at all, until very recently. It was long trenchcoats, with fishing hats and a pile of albums under the arm at Manchester Free Trade Hall.

That kind of conjures up our fans. They're loyal. And they go back a long way.

We were the last band to come out of the back page of the *Melody Maker* period. You used to be able to say "Who do I want to see tonight — Cream, Ten Years After, Genesis, Yes?" or whatever. You could go to any club, or college, and there'd be someone good on.

Bands would work up through clubs and colleges and universities, that was the way it was done — it was the respectable way to do it. The fact that it didn't happen very quickly for us certainly didn't bother me.

It didn't bother any of us, we just knew that it was the way it should be done. It was a way of investing in our future.

The thirty people you played to at the Wake Arms, Epping would become fifty the next time, and then they would tell their mates and so on.

That's what's different about bands today. They don't play the clubs and colleges and universities. There's a much quicker turnover of groups.

●PETER: We weren't quite dedicated enough to being on the road. Strat always used to talk about ivory towers, and he was probably right.

I felt that I had a responsibility to try and steer us towards being more accessible.

TONY: To me there was music and there was the career — the idea of 'making it' in different places. I always wanted to do it on our own terms — I never wanted to compromise. I think this feeling was shared by most of the members of the group.

I felt that we could easily have had a hit single. I still really think we could have had one. At the same time, we really wanted to try and get the music across which was far more difficult, yet we seemed to be quite successful at it without compromising ourselves.

■**After a second American tour in the spring, Genesis came off the road having toured consistently for two years and set time aside to prepare their next album. Meanwhile a live album, 'Genesis Live' was released in August 1973.**

●PHIL: We rehearsed at the same two places as we had done for 'Foxtrot' — Una Billing's School Of Dancing in Shepherd's Bush and at this doctor's house in Chessington. The doctor had six daughters and lots of dachshunds and between them the daughters and the dachshunds drove us mad.

We seemed to be spreading ourselves all over the place and it wasn't really coming together that well.

There was a suggestion from Charisma that as this was taking such a long time and there was a chance we'd miss the dead-line, that we should release a live album compiled from the best of the King Biscuit Hour tapes of recordings we'd made of our last tour.

This was the first Genesis live album. Up until then, we never actually felt that we sounded as good live as we did on record. In fact it was the reverse — we always sounded more gutsy on stage than we did on record.

●TONY: The writing period for 'Selling England' was a very long, drawn-out affair. It was the first time that we actually set time aside to write an album.

When we first went there, we had some magical days, and it all seemed to really go well. Then we hit a period when nothing seemed to happen; we just went over the same bits again.

We ended up working over some sections with a fine toothcomb — for instance, the penultimate part of 'Dancing With The Moonlit Knight', which is sort of stop, start, you know — and I began to think, "Is this really worth it?"

We got very frustrated — I seem to remember Phil in particular went through a very bad time during this period.

●MIKE: We probably wrote half of what we actually used in the first two weeks. I think we were given three months to write it, which was the kiss of death because it became such an open-ended thing.

It is an album which, for me, has got probably more highs and lows than any other album. For example, 'Battle Of Epping Forest' is an odd song — a fantastic backing track, a great vocal line, great lyrics; but together there's just too much happening. It's something we'd been guilty of in the past, but it came to a head in this track.

'Cinema Show', which I think is one of our strongest things, was put together by Tony, Phil and I. I wrote the acoustic song, and then we all wrote the solo.

●TONY: 'Cinema Show', was an example of extended playing. Mike, Phil and I were in a room together and Mike came out with a riff in 7/8, which had a great feel, and, by restricting his playing a little he allowed me to make the chord changes.

I like to play with chords because I've got a better feel for harmony than I have for melody.

So with Mike just hitting the bottom three or four strings of the guitar I managed to write endless bits on the rhythm. Just before we came to do the album, we put them in order, and the final section of 'Cinema Show' developed.

Mike and I wrote the lyrics to 'Cinema Show.' The first part, at least, is a fairly close rendition of a section of *The Wasteland* by T S Eliot. The idea of using the two words 'Romeo' and 'Juliet' actually was Peter's. I thought it should be more impersonal just using 'young clerk', or something, and I wasn't too sure about it to begin with.

In fact it worked quite well. Pete didn't like the lyric at all. He felt that we were out of our depth. But I think he was wrong.

In fact the lyrics on 'Firth Of Fifth', which is on the same album, is one of the worst set of lyrics I've been involved with. It's not just a question of being obscure, I really don't think it has anything going for it. Whereas 'Cinema Show' worked really well.

The main creation on this album was the 'Battle Of Epping Forest'. It's a pity it doesn't quite work because it really did sound good in the rehearsal room. But by the time we got the final version on record, there was a just a bit too much going on.

● PHIL: 'The Battle Of Epping Forest' just has too many words per minute.

If we had worked on the lyrics beforehand, or if there'd been a melody to start with, we could have said, "Hang on, we'll take a breather here."

As it is, you end up having to take the record off to have a burst of oxygen before you can listen to the next track! It literally left Pete out of breath on stage quite regularly: although he did sing it with a stocking over his head — which didn't help matters!

● PETER: I really got carried away with the lyrics for 'Battle Of Epping Forest'. I enjoyed writing them, but they didn't fit the music and by that point it was too late in the day.

What happened was that I insisted on doing most of the words as I thought I could do them better than the others — which, I think, was true. The problem was that I was incredibly slow, so that, often, by the time they saw the lyrics, they would have done their parts.

The backing tracks would be complete but there were no melodies and no words.

● TONY: I think this was the first time that I didn't worry too much what the others thought if I played bum notes. To be unself-conscious about your playing in front of the other members of the group is very important, I think — in order to let ideas flow freely.

● MIKE: A lot of our writing has come from jamming. However, jamming on stage is not the same as jamming together in rehearsal rooms. This all comes back, I think, to personalities.

Nowadays when we jam on stage, I'm very relaxed and we make up quite a few bits as we go along.

There was a long jamming section in 'The Lamb'. In the rehearsal room, in front of Tony and Phil, Pete and Steve, I could jam for hours. We'd all play countless wrong notes and just do anything we wanted.

But we couldn't jam on stage. I'm saying this to contradict any idea that we were a tight band all of the time. On stage we were, because we weren't relaxed enough to jam. But, as I said, during a lot of the rehearsals we'd jam for three or four hours a day.

● PETER: There were points at which I felt that as a band, we all worked very well together. The highpoints for me were the end of 'Cinema Show' and the 9/8 section in 'Supper's Ready'. I had nothing to do with generating them, but I still felt very good about them.

There were other elements however, which troubled me. I was still having difficulty communicating with people, particularly if it was anything that was in some way emotional.

● MIKE: I think we were getting conscious of technique on this album, or very aware of the fact that we'd become quite well-known for our techniques as musicians. The fact that we'd become competent players gave us confidence to play fast phrases, and to be clever.

There's a bit of that on the album, I think, and there are some moments when we're all trying to be too clever. But at the same time, you've got to try for something, to move on to the next stage.

● STEVE: I managed to develop my style throughout the course of the album even though my marriage was about to break up. The band was my lifeline. I never felt closer to the band than I felt then. Genesis was my relief from the very difficult domestic trauma that I was going through.

● PETER: We were conscious of America at that time because I remember thinking that we were going to get knocked in England for slanting stuff towards America, which was partly why I wanted the title, 'Selling England By The Pound'.

■ 'Selling England By The Pound' came out in October 1973 and got to number three. In April 1974, Genesis made their first appearance in the singles charts when 'I Know What I Like (In Your Wardrobe)' reached number twenty-one.

● TONY: 'I Know What I Like' came from a riff that Steve had been playing for years. We just jammed on it for hours during some of the better days when making this album.

I think the day it really took off was when I was playing the fuzz electric piano and the organ. The electric piano was slightly out of tune with the organ, and the effect was just amazing.

Pete was making funny noises into a mike, and we were working out a melody line for the verse.

I think we probably felt at the time that it had single potential but we also accepted we had very little idea about singles and we never aimed for them anyhow.

● STEVE: It was a riff that I'd been playing with Phil, right back at the time of 'Foxtrot', which the rest of the band felt was too Beatle-ish. We just kept on playing it and it became 'I Know What I Like'.

We used to joke about it as our hit single. Everyone used to say, "Oh, pass the hit single please, will you."

We sat around and Pete and Phil jammed a vocal which developed from something on the guitar, and it was transformed from something which sounded a little too much like the Beatles to something which sounded a lot like Genesis.

It became the first little bit of plastic which got anywhere in the charts.

● PETER: We'd always tried to avoid writing hits, which may sound a really dumb thing. Ac-

PAUL CANTY/LFI

□ *1975.*

tually now, I think it was really dumb.

Tony played that melody line, and although I didn't think it was a great melody line, I knew people would like it.

The verse, I think, is good. I don't dislike the chorus but I felt, at the time, that it was taking the easy way.

We did have these very high ideals about trying to do things a different way, avoiding clichés wherever possible. Although we did secretly borrow from people at different times.

■ **Chart success had not reduced the band's debts to Charisma. Tony Stratton-Smith had been handling the band's affairs although others such as Marcus Bicknell, Adrian Selby and Ed Goodgold had attempted to manage them with varying degrees of success. Tony Smith (no relation), a successful promoter who had worked on the 'Six Bob' tour back in 1971, was appointed the band's 'official' manager in October 1973.**

● TONY: We didn't break even until 'Trick Of The Tail' — up until that point, we were subsidised by Charisma.

MIKE: We used to meet and talk money. It was getting ridiculous because you couldn't make that sort of figure mean anything to you. It didn't really matter because you would never leave the group and actually owe the money. It wasn't recoupable. But I wasn't crazy about it, you know!

● PHIL: I remember reading that we were £150,000 in debt. But it wasn't us, you see, it wasn't Mike, Tony, Pete and I that owed the money, it was Genesis.

● MIKE: In America, we were still managed by a guy called Ed Goodgold, who also managed Sha-Na-Na. He only managed us in America when we actually got out there. He never had any money; he spent his whole time trying to raise money for the next plane fare.

It couldn't have been an easy job; there was a tour that year which both Ed Goodgold and Tony Smith helped to manage. Tony Smith, however, brought about a real change. The production side of things had become a big headache because it was so disorganised. Tony changed that in just over a year which was a big help to us, because it meant we could stop worrying about the production and management.

I had got involved in the management of tours. I had a flat in Weymouth Street, and Adrian Selby slept on the floor next door. There were no proper beds and the office was our flat — my flat.

I ended up telephoning America at all hours of the night to ask about sound and lights and that sort of thing. It was chaotic. We set off for one tour in America and lost a guy at Heathrow Airport — he went missing, along with a load of equipment, for a day and a half. Then we arrived in Montreal to change planes, and lost our lighting operator. We eventually got to Quebec with two or three people missing. It was that kind of tour. You were always worrying about whether the lights were going to fall on you and kill you, and whether things were going to blow up. Tony Smith took that responsibility off our shoulders, and he actually started to hassle record companies and people like that.

● PHIL: We were obviously becoming more and more popular, but we didn't have amazing record deals and stuff; we were still only earning about £35 a week. Tony saw all this and wanted to try and help us, I think. Up until a couple of years ago we didn't have a management contract with him. He worked for that length of time on trust.

■ **By mid-1974, Peter, Tony, Steve, Mike and Phil had been together for four years.**

● PETER: Tony and I knew each other very well by now, and we were a combination of best friends and worst enemies. Like any long-term relationship, as with a married couple for instance, you get to know each other's Achilles' heel. You turn the screw and you know exactly how to pulverise the opposition. He was slightly better at it than me largely because he had a better defence mechanism. It was all part and parcel of our relationship, which included moments that were really positive and good.

I felt very easy with Phil. There were times at some gigs when we used to go into a room to get away from it all and sit down together at a piano. My piano playing was humble, and, at that point, Phil's was even more humble.

We used to sing with each other and get into grooves. He was very much into an American style of singing, a soft Richie Havens — the type of singing that you can still hear in some of his songs today, my style was quite different, a sort of weird English thing — the way I sounded on 'Willow Farm' in the middle of 'Supper's Ready', or 'Harold The Barrel' or whatever.

They were great moments. I think we would both fantasise then about making music on our own, or doing things together.

I felt that Mike and I could talk things through and change positions or at least admit to being seen to change positions. Tony was more insecure in some ways, and could not be seen to let go of what he'd originally argued for.

This is what really interests me when I see other bands — their internal structure. It's interesting to observe any group of people that are functioning as a collaborative team on a creative project as there's always an immense

WARING ABBOTT

□ *1976, enter Bill Bruford.*

amount of ego manipulation.

Phil could be a terrible coward. I had originally asserted a lot of influence over the choice of a new drummer and, at the time, I had felt that I got a sort of soul brother in the band, in terms of feel.

When there were arguments, I would look to Phil, as I thought that he would be in support of what I was saying, and he would sit on the fence, and refuse to budge.

Other times, when he was basically in support of Tony's position and opposed to me, he would still be afraid of committing himself.

Tony was always the most difficult about having his stuff rejected. We'd all submit bits, and people would only like a certain number of them. After he'd stormed out of the room twice, you didn't want another major explosion from him, so you'd say, "OK, Tony, let's go with that."

Then Phil would have to work very hard to try and loosen up Tony's stuff. Mike's stuff tended — and my stuff too, I think — to have more feel to it. But Tony used to come up with some great melodies.

There were moments socially when we still had a lot of fun. But, once we got down to the serious business...phew!

I think it forced people to come up with some really good stuff, because they knew if it didn't work, it was going to get shot down. You were at risk of being slaughtered. I think the only person who managed to get away with things that not everyone liked, was Tony!

I was machiavellian and manipulative about trying to get my way.

●TONY: I used to get really moody if I felt very strongly about something and someone else argued about it. More often than not, I'd storm out of the room and go for a walk.

Phil was amazed, I think, when he first joined the band, he'd never seen this sort of thing before — the kind of violence that we used to get up to with each other.

However, I never hold grudges for any length of time. After five minutes I would tell myself, "What a fool", and then, after about half an hour, I would have made it up with whoever it was.

Most people accept me as just being that kind of person. I tend to have those scenes less often now, but there are still times when they occur, largely, I think, out of frustration.

After 'Foxtrot' I suddenly got confident about the things I was writing. The things I wanted to do most, suddenly seemed appropriate for the band.

I had a lot of material up my sleeve, and I felt I could have written a whole album's worth without any trouble at all. At last I was able to get it across to other members of the group rather better that I had before.

●STEVE: Phil and I were frankly more earthy than the others. I always thought that Mike had an amazing sense of humour, he often us-

□ *1976.*

ed to have me in stitches. I think I had the most respect for Tony, which didn't necessarily mean that we saw eye to eye on everything — in fact, far from it.

There were a lot of clashes, and a lot of times when I used to feel that everybody else was wrong. They were just a bunch of toughs with a veneer of respectability. They really were very tough and single minded about what they did. A lot of people bit the dust along the way, but, I really do think, in hindsight, it was just too bad. The end justified the means.

I can't remember ever really unburdening myself emotionally to the other guys because there was always too much at stake. This is something that has a lot to do with success and, in particular, with combined success. You are, by necessity, helping each other, but you are competing with each other as well.

The competitive element had the negative side effect of allowing many things to go unsaid.

And I suddenly realised that the only way to survive was by being self-sufficient emotionally. I began to keep myself to myself; although we'd hang out together every day and laugh and joke, I'd keep my innermost feelings hidden.

●PHIL: We always used to have strong territorial rights about who played what. I remember recording 'I Know What I Like' and, while Tony was away for an afternoon, Peter had an idea, switched Tony's gear on, played and recorded it. Tony came in the next day and we played the track, and he said, "What's that?" Pete said, "That's a mellotron thing I did last night." And Tony said, "I'm the keyboard player." Pete started to argue and

sparks flew. Someone else probably walked out. The usual story.

There's always been this thing about people's territories and I'm sure that's why Peter eventually decided to leave. He was writing stuff on the piano that he wanted to play.

●PETER: There was always a problem about people not coming clean with who was best at doing what. We were not able to own up to it. If we had been able to do that, and had been mature enough to avoid these petty squabbles, the band would have worked a lot better.

After I left, and later when Steve had left, there was a period when people could relax. There was one less person to argue with, and because there was less fighting, the production end of it could run much more smoothly.

I think one of the major changes which began to happen towards the end of the time I was there, and which has definitely happened since, is that the band learnt how to make the best of the material through production, arrangement and performance.

On many of those early albums we had some material that was not given a chance because we were inept at recognising its strong points and making those work.

I feel that Genesis could have broken through to much bigger audiences had we found ourselves a charismatic producer, rather than using a sort of laid-back engineer-type producer.

I really felt that, if we could find the right charismatic producer with a strong enough personality and a good enough sense of music, that they could, as an outsider, help us make the right decisions regarding the material.

I couldn't do it as I was obviously prejudiced. I had my bits, and if I said that I didn't think someone else's bit worked, then they would say that a bit of mine didn't work. Ridiculous, petty band politics.

It was a pretty unattractive role for anyone to take on as it would have meant really upsetting people as well as getting upset yourself. It was almost like a religion — through our muddled, neurotic, paranoid processes, we'd arrived at this thing which was called music, and to challenge it, at that point, was like questioning someone's religious beliefs. And yet, we needed it; I longed for that person to come along.

Genesis was a collaborative venture — a co-operative — all the royalties were being split equally, and there was quite a lot of idealism.

And then, suddenly, I was being singled out as the front man, the performer. I was doing the interviews. People assumed that I did all the writing.

In order to try and redress the balance, I played down my role. When people said they wrote songs, what they often meant was that they wrote the chord sequences. Again, if the melodies and the lyrics were put down afterwards by me or someone else, that would not be construed as part of the songwriting.

I used to swallow a lot of that because it was clearly pointed out to me that I was getting an unfair share of the credit from the outside world. All that was reversed after I left, and the band still managed to make music that satisfied all the fans. As a result, people probably assumed that I hadn't written any of the music!

I think I had the benefit of the excitement of being the front man. But the penalty for that was that, within the band, there was a hotbed of resentment towards me, which was never openly declared.

As a result, I was not treated very sympathetically. In other words, they were less prepared to give me space to do things, as they felt that I'd already got more space than I deserved.

■ **That summer, Genesis started work on their most ambitious project so far — a concept album, 'The Lamb Lies Down On Broadway'.**

● PETER: Several ideas for the album were presented in order for the band to exercise a democratic vote. I knew mine was the strongest and I knew it would win — or, I knew that I could get it to win.

The only other idea that was seriously considered was *The Little Prince* which Mike was in favour of — a kids' story. I thought that was too twee. This was 1974; it was pre-punk but I still thought we needed to base the story around a contemporary figure rather than a fantasy creation. We were beginning to get into the era of the big, fat supergroups of the seventies and I thought, "I don't want to go down with this Titanic".

Once the story idea had been accepted we had all these heavy arguments about writing the lyrics. My argument was that there aren't many novels which are written by a committee. I said, "I think this is something that only I'm going to be able to get into, in terms of understanding the characters and the situations". I wrote indirectly about lots of my emotional experiences in 'The Lamb' and so I didn't want other people colouring it. In fact there are parts of it which are almost indecipherable and very difficult which I don't think are very successful.

In some ways it was quite a traditional concept album — it was a type of *Pilgrim's Progress* but with this street character in leather jacket and jeans.

Rael would have been called a punk at that time without all the post-'76 connotations. The Ramones hadn't started then, although the New York Dolls had, but they were more glam-punk. 'The Lamb' was looking towards *West Side Story* as a starting point.

● MIKE: It was about a greasy Puerto Rican kid! For once we were writing about subject matter which was neither airy-fairy, nor romantic. We finally managed to get away from writing about unearthly things which I think helped the album.

● TONY: All the lyrics were written by Peter, apart from one or two tracks, because he'd thought up the story line. He didn't really want anyone else to do it.

We also had a lot of work to do, because we had decided by that time that we were going to make a double album.

This meant there was a division as Pete went off and wrote the lyrics, and everyone else wrote the music.

By the time Pete had finished the lyrics, there were about two or three holes where there wasn't a song, and we needed to write something. 'Carpet Crawlers' was one and the 'Grand Parade Of Lifeless Packaging' was another.

● MIKE: I think that 'The Lamb' is one of our best albums — one of our most different, anyway. We started writing, and it just came out very easily. After the previous album, it was a big relief.

We realised quite quickly that we had three good sides — not just two good sides and another side, but three good sides. So we had to go for a double.

Pete started the lyrics, and it finally became apparent we hadn't got a chance in hell of getting it finished by the deadline.

● PHIL: We were living at Headley Grange — this house that Led Zeppelin, Bad Company and the Pretty Things had lived in. It was a bit of a shambles — in fact they'd ripped the shit out of it. We were all living together and writing together and it went very well to start with.

Pete had said he wanted to do all the words so Mike and Tony had backed off and we were merrily churning out this music. Every time we sat down and played, something good came out.

● PETER: Around the time we started work on 'The Lamb' I had this call from Hollywood from William Friedkin who'd seen the story I'd written on the back of the live album and he thought it indicated a weird, visual mind. He was trying to put together a sci-fi film and he wanted to get a writer who'd never been involved with Hollywood before.

We were working at Headley Grange which I felt was partly haunted by Jimmy Page's black magic experiments, and was full of rock and roll legend. I would go bicycle to the phone box down the hill and dial Friedkin in California with pockets stuffed full of 10p pieces.

● PHIL: Suddenly Peter came up and said, "Do you mind if we stop for a bit", and we all said, "No. Of course we don't want to stop." It was a matter of principle more than anything else. So he said, "OK, I want to do the film, so I'm leaving."

I remember we were sitting in the garden by the porch saying, "What are we going to do? We'll carry on. We'll have an instrumental group", which for five minutes was a serious idea because we had a lot of music written.

● TONY: We were just going to carry on. We were going to write another story line. Not that I wanted Pete to leave because he was a very strong contributor and I really enjoyed working with him.

I felt that the group needed all the energy we could possibly put into it because we still had a long way to go career-wise, and I thought musically it was still very interesting.

If you are going to do it properly there's no way that one person can suddenly go off like that leaving the rest to hang about for three months. We made that very clear and that's why he left.

It was all getting a little tedious, because the group was very much the main thing in our lives at that particular time.

Peter kept saying if this William Friedkin offer came, he would do that in preference to working with us. And I thought, "This is absurd."

There came a point when he decided to write a screenplay, so he left for a bit. Anyhow, higher authorities stepped in — I think it was Strat — to try and keep us together.

So Peter made a definite commitment to finish the album before he did anything else. But I think it made all of us feel that he was getting fed up and it was only a matter of time before he left.

● MIKE: If you push Pete into a corner, he will retreat still further. When we tried to tie him down, he just became more vague. He went off back home to Bath...and that was it. We carried on writing and didn't really think very far ahead.

● PETER: Another thing that rubbed the band up the wrong way was that Tangerine Dream were going to do the film score for Friedkin. The others thought I was using the group as a springboard to jump off for my own personal success and wasn't even bringing them along with me. But Friedkin didn't want Genesis. He only wanted me for weird ideas, not for music. I just wanted a month to do this script outline. So I walked out. There was a big eruption with Charisma and I think Strat had to come out of his watering hole to help resolve it.

● MIKE: Eventually, I rang Pete one morning and said, "Well, this is silly. Come back, and we'll sort it out." So he came back, and we picked up where we left off.

Slowly, as the album progressed, William Friedkin's project became more and more vague. But once that sort of thing happens, the seeds of discontent are sown.

● PETER: I had said, "If you are not going to allow me to do anything else I'm not going to stay." And Mike had replied, "If you delay the project, we can reach an agreement."

In a sense, I'd won that round, but the resentment which had already accumulated became even more pronounced.

They were definitely nervous about carrying on without me. Yet they have proved they could because the band has become a lot bigger than when I was in it.

In reality, they shouldn't have been worried. I think I had more confidence in their ability to manage without me than they did because I knew that in the long run, songwriting was what really mattered. And they are good songwriters.

● PHIL: Pete came back after a week because I think Friedkin got frightened at the idea of being the cause of breaking up the group. He told Pete that he didn't want *that* much of a commitment, just a few ideas.

So Pete found himself, from what I gather, without the job and came back with his tail between his legs. Things were restored to normal but, from that moment on, I think we all felt that this could happen again at any time.

● TONY: Pete came back and we finished the album, and I really enjoyed it.

We used a lot of moods — at times things were little more than improvisations on an idea. For instance, Mike would say, "Pharoahs going down the Nile" and he would just play two chords and instantly the rest of us would conjure up that particular mood. That one ended up on the album as 'Fly On A Windshield'.

We did that with lots of the other tracks. The best jam we had in the rehearsal room ended

1976.

up being called 'The Waiting Room', which we called 'The Evil Jam'. We switched off all the lights and just made noises. And the first time it really was frightening.

PHIL: 'The Evil Jam' started with Steve inventing noises and Tony messing around on a couple of synthesizers — we were just mucking about with some really nasty sounds.

We were all getting very intense; Peter was blowing his oboe reeds into the microphone and playing his flute with the echoplex on when suddenly there was this great clap of thunder and it started raining.

We all thought, "We've got in contact with something heavy here." It was about five or six in the evening and we were making all these weird noises when the thunderstorm started and it began to pour down. And then we all shifted gear and got into a really melodic mood.

At moments like that it really was a five-piece thing. We worked well together on 'The Lamb' — the two albums gave us the room to do it.

After we had prepared all our material, we went to another house in Wales to record. We put down the backing tracks in two weeks, and a month later we were still waiting for the words. Peter was well behind. Then he started saying, "I need another piece of music to link these two songs."

We got bored with it in the end and nobody could help him because he was determined to do it on his own.

PETER: I was pretty good at manipulating but I think by 'The Lamb' the resentment towards me was so big that I had very little space. And I felt the only way I could work was to go into a corner and function on my own. A lot of the melodies were written after the event — after the backing tracks had been put down.

PHIL: We ended up back in London doing the vocals and mixing the album in shifts. I'd be mixing and overdubbing all night and then Tony and Mike would come in and remix what I'd done because I'd lost all semblance of normality by that point.

Finally it seemed as if we'd been through hell and high water just to get it out. It certainly wasn't one of my favourite albums at the time but I can see now that it's one of our better recordings. We were still suffering from bad production up to that point, I think.

MIKE: I think a lot of people were put off by the idea of a concept, this idea of it all hanging together. When it came out, it was a commercial failure. People talk about it now as a Genesis classic, but at the time, it died a death.

STEVE: I was an innocent bystander on 'The Lamb'. It happened despite me, not with me.

REX FEATURES

☐ *Chester.*

All the things that I'd managed to hold back on 'Selling England By The Pound' seemed to come back in full force here.

The nightmarishly long sides — everything linked to everything else. I really felt it was very indulgent. I couldn't quite get to grips with it or contribute something great in a guitar sense.

I don't think Tony's ever done a finer album. But I did feel the amount of stuff I was managing to put across was painfully small. My marriage, at this point, was also on the rocks.

■ **'The Lamb Lies Down On Broadway' was eventually released in November 1974 and reached number ten the following month. The planned world tour to present the concept live was delayed when Steve injured his hand.**

● STEVE: I was at an Alex Harvey gig one night, and there were all these pressures mounting up — my domestic crisis, the band crisis. The upshot was that I got extremely drunk at the reception afterwards and heard someone say, "You know, the band would be nothing without Alex." I suddenly saw red, it was as if somebody had said, "The band would be nothing without Pete."

I had a wine glass in my hand, and before I knew it, I'd crushed the glass. I was rushed off to hospital; I'd almost cut my thumb off, it was that bad.

They stitched me up, and did a pretty good job under the circumstances, although later I had to have it re-opened and operated on. Things seemed to be going really badly for me — going back out on the road proved to be the saving grace for me, as I was able to immerse myself totally in my work again. Playing 'The Lamb' on stage was nothing compared with the emotional experience of putting the thing together. It calmed me down.

● PHIL: I can't remember too much about 'The Lamb' tour. That was my grass tour. I sank beneath my headphones every night to play the whole of 'The Lamb' and thoroughly enjoyed myself!

We had to play the entire album which was pretty gruelling, especially in America, because the album wasn't out there when we started touring. We played two hours of completely new music and a couple of tunes which they knew at the end but by then it was too late.

● MIKE: It was a big mistake. We tired of 'The Lamb' tour much earlier than the others because we were tied down to playing the whole album — we were stuck with some sections that weren't great live, just because they were part of the story.

● TONY: I thought 'The Lamb' tour was very adventurous and had some very strong moments in it. But it was the *least* enjoyable of all the shows we've ever had to play. It was a very rigid show. You couldn't change the set.

The other problem was that the first half of the show was better which meant you had the weaker half to finish with.

There were an awful lot of props. It was a very theatrical show. But a lot of things went wrong. For instance, the slides were never right. I don't think there was a single show when all the slides worked perfectly.

● PHIL: The stage effects, if you look at the photographs now, were quite amazing. It wasn't a particularly expensive show to put on, but the mike cable would get caught, or Pete would be struggling to get the microphone into his Slipperman costume.

There was a time in Oslo when the flash-bomb went off, and blew the whole monitoring system up. Our production manager mixed too much bang, and not enough flash, so the whole thing exploded.

It was bloody dangerous, because I could hear bits flying past my head, and we had to stop playing in the middle of a song. The bloke poked his head round the curtain and said, "Sorry!"

I remember shouting at him, "You're fired! You're fired! Get out of here." And the audience all got up as one person, and filed out without a word.

I was starting to feel rather frustrated because I could play well or badly and no-one would really notice. That depressed me. The theatrical side was being talked about a lot and the music was very much secondary. That's when Brand X came on the scene, and made me think about leaving.

Then when Peter said he was leaving, it suddenly changed my attitude. I thought that maybe the theatrical side would have to go — not that I wanted to get rid of Pete. People would come in afterwards and steam straight past Tony, Mike, Steve and I, go straight up to Peter and say, "You're fantastic. We really enjoyed the show." It was becoming a one-man show to the audience.

■ **In December 1974, midway through 'The Lamb' tour, Peter decided to leave the group.**

● PETER: The pressure was accumulating. I was saying to myself, "OK, we get successful in America. We get rich. What then? Do we become like the other bands who've made it."

There were things about those groups that I didn't like, and I didn't want to become part of a supergroup. I was beginning to dislike myself for doing what I was doing.

I finally cracked in Cleveland. I went into Tony Smith's room and told him I was leaving and he tried to talk me out of it, saying, "Hold on a couple of days." I said that I'd been thinking about it a lot and that it was final.

The rest of the band were told a few days later in Canada. Their position was that we had worked eight years to get this far, and now, finally, we were about to make it and I was pulling the carpet out from underneath it all.

I felt terrible, but I knew that I'd made up my mind, and I can be really obstinate. I wanted a career where I had the opportunity to take on other projects but the band had this army-like attitude. There was no room to be flexible — if you were in the band, you were in it 100 per-cent, or you were out.

A lot of the friction towards the end arose because I wanted to follow up those opportunities and also, I was the first one to have kids. My first child spent three weeks in an incubator, and the doctors didn't think she was going to live.

Although there was sympathy, it held up recording schedules. The band didn't understand that. For me there was absolutely no question of priorities in a situation like that.

Now the others have kids they understand. This was one of the factors which helped me think, "This is not a lifestyle that I wish to continue."

I had no idea what I wanted to do, but I knew I was sick of rock, the business, and everything about it. I just wanted to get out.

● PHIL: Halfway through the tour, Peter said he was leaving. I remember we were in Manchester and he was being offered money just to finish the tour. I remember £3,000 being mentioned. And we all said, "Well, if he's having it, we want it — £3,000 each."

It wasn't to stay in the group or anything. It was just that he wanted to leave and there was obviously such a lot to lose. We had the tour booked and everything.

We were all getting on so well too. Our personal and professional lives were separate. It was 'us' and 'them' again. It was, "Will you stay in the group?", "I don't know", "Well, have a drink with me Pete."

● PETER: I was asked to tour Europe. And do more tours. I felt so guilty because I was allegedly destroying Genesis. At least, if we toured Europe, we could pay off most of our debts. Which wasn't the case — we were still in the red when I left.

● MIKE: Pete's personal life was suffering through touring and constant pressure. I think that having written all the lyrics on 'The Lamb', he would not have found it easy to go back to our previous method of songwriting. Perhaps he felt that 'The Lamb' was a good, final statement on which to leave.

● STEVE: It looked as though we couldn't dissuade Pete, so I wondered what I was going to do. I started writing some material on my own. I thought at the time, "this could be the beginning of my solo career whether I like it or not."

TERRY MURDEN

'Say It's Alright Joe', 1978.

I went to the studio and recorded 'The Voyage Of The Acolyte'. I didn't know whether I was going to come out with a bunch of outtakes, or whether it was going to be a whole album. But it turned into a complete album.

I was just glad to get it done, and I was even more pleased when it went silver. I hadn't felt that I was sufficiently well-known as an individual. I still wasn't doing very well in the guitar polls at that point.

So, I stuck with the band and trod water for a couple of years, if I'm quite honest about it.

● PHIL: I was tempted by another opportunity. I was offered the lady with the big tits — Brand X — as opposed to the staid wife which was Genesis.

Brand X started off as a real jamming band in stark contrast to Genesis where we used to tie things down.

I had been just as responsible for tying things down as everybody else had. Maybe I felt it was something that couldn't change so I wanted to get out and do something different.

■ **Peter played his last gig with Genesis at St Etienne in France in May 1975. He retired from the rock scene for nearly two years before embarking on a solo career.**

● TONY: At Pete's final gig, he played 'The Last Post' in the dressing-room — on the oboe, which he never really fathomed.

I think for people associated with the group — wives, girlfriends and friends — it was really depressing. It was definitely the end of an era if not the end of the band.

However the rest of us had been talking quite a bit and we were fairly keen to go on. We thought we could cope with it. It was definitely a strange period.

● PETER: I had a big lump in my throat when we did the last gigs in France. A big chapter in my life was coming to an end, and I couldn't tell anyone. We had a policy of doing no interviews throughout that tour, but quite often people said, "We'll only give you space if we can talk to Peter." Which didn't help matters at all.

I felt a real sham — I couldn't tell people what was going on. But I'd made an agreement, because I felt so guilty, that I would keep quiet about it until the band had time to sort themselves out.

I saw Genesis again at the Hammersmith Odeon on the next tour. I felt much more at ease than I had expected to, except that I got some twitches in 'Supper's Ready'; it looked like somebody else dressed up in my entrails.

Now I can watch Phil sing without feeling emotionally attached to a song. I always enjoy watching the interaction between him and Chester on drums.

1975-1981

Tony, Mike, Steve and Phil started preparing a new album during the summer of 1975, without having recruited a new singer.

● PHIL: As soon as Pete said he was leaving, we knew we were going to carry on. We were making plans in hotel bedrooms. We agreed to have a couple of months off after 'The Lamb' tour, write some songs, and then meet up to play what we'd written.

We'd made a verbal agreement with Peter that he wouldn't tell anybody he was leaving, to give us a chance to get something under our belt. If anybody had got wind of him leaving, it would have been the obituary columns for Genesis.

In fact, we had already got material prepared for a new album. We put an advert in the papers saying that we wanted a singer. A lot of people sent in tapes, and the office sifted through most of them as there were a lot of jokers — people sending in Frank Sinatra songs.

It was amazing, some of these people were singing along to Genesis tracks — you could hear the record in the background. Mick Rogers came from Manfred Mann, he was basically a guitarist who sang. But we only wanted singers. Nick Lowe sent a tape in.

In the end we saw about 50 people. But whenever we liked someone's voice it was because it sounded like Pete's.

We eventually settled on one bloke we liked and we went to the studio with him.

One of the earliest backing tracks we had was 'Squonk'. So we went to the first session with this bloke, and he went downstairs and started singing 'Squonk' out of key and I walked out! I thought, "Good sense will prevail here!"

There was nothing wrong with him. It was just that he was nervous and it was the wrong key for his voice.

Next day, I came in and I said, "Listen, I wouldn't mind a crack at it," because deep down I really wanted to have a go. And they said, "Fine," because I'd sung on our albums, but I didn't have a 'ballsy' voice, as far as anybody knew.

I had always sung the more angelic stuff, I'd never really had to push my voice to do the heavy parts. I started to sing and the first line was 'Like father, like son...,' and everybody started to perk up.

So we proceeded verse by verse through 'Squonk' and when the next song came up, they said, "Have a crack at this one." Suddenly we'd done all the songs, and we still didn't have a singer. I'd done the album.

● TONY: We started off with the idea that maybe Phil would sing 'Ripples' and possibly something else. Slowly it dawned on us that we weren't going to find another singer. We had got someone in who had sung 'Squonk', but the pitch was totally wrong for him.

I was actually ill the evening he did the recording. I came in the next morning and said, "You're joking." They agreed that it was absolutely terrible. It wasn't his fault.

Phil had a go at it. It immediately sounded a lot better, and once he'd done that, we decided to let him try the whole thing.

We were all very proud of ourselves and pleased that we'd done it as a four-piece. It was a very happy album to make. At that time we all felt like underdogs.

We actually had a serious producer for the first time. Dave Hentschel gave us a really fresh feel. Recording 'Trick Of The Tail' proved to be the most fun of all our albums.

When 'Dance On A Volcano' came together I thought it was magic, it had happened so spontaneously.

'Los Endos' revealed Phil's influence on the band. He'd been into jazz-rock and suggested taking a bit from a song called 'It's Yourself' which appeared on the B side of a single. We just played the basic riff and the idea of developing it came naturally. In many ways, it's the most adventurous track on the album.

I knew we could write good music without Peter. Any one of us could have left and the rest would still have written good music.

● MIKE: 'Trick' was a very neat album. I really felt there were no weak moments. I've got my favourite tracks, but at no point have I ever looked back and thought, "Well, that wasn't a great song."

● PHIL: Here we were writing 'Squonk' and 'Dance On A Volcano' when I saw *Melody Maker* and there was Peter on the front — 'Gabriel quits Genesis.' Someone had got wind of it.

There we were on the front page 'Rest in Peace. They were a great group.' It was ridiculous. The four of us had just recorded a good album and were saying, "Wait till they hear this." And they were writing obituaries.

● MIKE: All the post-mortems and the 'they were good in their day' statements came out. It really shook us for a week or so because we'd forgotten that the public did not know what was about to happen.

We kept meeting people and it was so difficult to explain, even to friends. I found myself saying, "This is great, it's fantastic" and it sounded as if I was desperate. I stopped saying anything until the album came out and spoke for itself. Then there was a great reaction — a sudden backlash the other way. It was a good opportunity for people to reappraise us. It's not often you can actually relisten to a group, and feel there's enough change to be able to revise your opinion.

But even after we'd done the album, we were still looking for a singer. At that point, we still regarded Phil as drummer. It was never a case of "Oh good, there's Phil. I hope it'll be OK." He slowly took on the role of singer on the album, it just happened naturally. I didn't like to suggest Phil as a permanent solution as I wasn't sure he wanted to give up contact with the drums. But he suggested it, and it fell into place.

● TONY: We were still thinking of getting a singer for our live shows, and then Phil said he wanted to do it — and said he'd find another drummer.

Mike and I had thought of this before, and we didn't think that Phil would ever agree to it as he was first and foremost a drummer.

● PHIL: I think it was my wife who suggested that I take on the singer's role. I said, "No, I'm not going to come out from behind the drums. I like drumming. You must be joking!"

Anyway, I suggested it to the other guys in the band, and they had much the same reaction but, after a while, they thought it wasn't such a silly idea. That meant I had to find another drummer. Around that time, I was doing gigs with Brand X, and Bill Bruford was playing with them on percussion. We were both at a Brand X rehearsal, and during a break, he said, "I hear that you're singing in the band now — so who's playing drums?"

I replied, "We haven't got anybody. I'm still trying to find someone." He said, "Well, what about me?" So I said, "You don't want to do that, do you? You've done it all with Yes and King Crimson."

He said, "Actually, I would quite like it." So I replied, "Come down and have a go."

He came and met the band and got on well with everybody straight away. And for the time being our problems were over.

■ **Bill Bruford was born in May, 1950 in Sevenoaks. He was educated at Tonbridge Public School and played with Yes from 1968 to 1972 and King Crimson from 1972 to 1974.**

● BILL: I was rehearsing with Brand X — I was playing percussion and Phil was on drums. During a break, Phil mentioned they had a 'small problem' with Genesis, namely that Gabriel had left. They'd been auditioning singers because Phil reckoned none of the fifty or so that they'd heard were as good as he was.

I said, "You sing and I'll play drums". He thought that was a good idea because he wanted someone who could play a bit like him so that he could rely on the drums behind him.

The group seemed to accept this as a temporary solution prior to either finding a permanent drummer or deciding that Phil was a hopeless singer after a dozen gigs. But this was never the case. Phil had been to drama school when he was a kid which meant he was able to feel his way easily around the stage, right from his very first gig as a singer. It was a very competent performance.

I'd never seen the band with Peter in it, but I'd always liked Phil's drumming. It always seemed to me that Phil was the most musical person in the band. I felt Genesis were a bit derivative of Yes and King Crimson until Peter's character started coming through more.

When I joined it was a closed shop in the writing department. It was clear to me that I was expected to play and nothing more. I didn't want to interfere with a five-year writing partnership; it didn't seem right to steam in and start making suggestions about what they should and shouldn't do.

■ **'Trick Of The Tail' was released in February 1976. It got to number three in the charts — their biggest selling album so far. Phil made his debut as singer in the group in March 1976 at London, Ontario, at the start of the North American tour.**

PHIL: I remember going to the first gig scared stiff, not about the singing, but about talking to the audience. Peter used to tell these funny stories between each song which amused the crowd and covered up a lot of tuning and instrument changes. But as soon as I'd started, the audience was so warm they must have known how nervous we were all feeling. After the first tune, everything settled down, and it was fine.

After a while people started saying, "How come your voice sounds a lot like Pete's?" But I wasn't actually trying to make it sound like anybody.

If there were any harmonies involved on our albums it was usually me singing them. And on some of the songs like 'I Know What I Like', there were usually two voices singing all the time. You got used to the sound of our vocals, so if you took half away, the other half sounded very similar. My voice was there, but people always thought it was Pete's.

● TONY: Phil was a more natural singer than Pete. Pete was more contrived as a singer. I've always loved Pete's voice but I wished that he would let his voice be more natural.

Phil has a very pure voice which has got better and better over the years.

I was surprised how easy it was for us after 'Trick Of The Tail' and I was also surprised by the acceptance of Phil on stage. The album sold far more than 'The Lamb'.

I thought this was crazy. I mean, people had always behaved towards the group as if Peter was Genesis. We made one album without him and suddenly it wasn't a problem. I knew the album was good but it seemed almost too easy really.

And when we started touring again, no-one ever said, "Where's Pete?" Perhaps people gave Phil a chance because he was one of the group — they didn't want to be antagonistic towards someone who had always been a member of the band.

● MIKE: The band changed in terms of how the audience saw us because Pete had always been such a mysterious, untouchable figure. Phil was very much the boy next door. We had always appeared rather cold on stage and he broke down that barrier by being humourous and cheeky.

God, he's been called cheeky so many times in reviews, but it is actually how he comes across. If there's someone putting that kind of mischief across, it's hard to take things too seriously, which I think is good for us.

● PHIL: I'm glad that I've been able to achieve a one to one relationship with our audiences. I think they see me as more of a regular bloke; without the mysterious, remote qualities that Pete had. Although it could have worked against us because Peter undeniably had something very special.

I think it's nice when you can crack a joke and make yourself look an idiot. It deflates any kind of pomp. It's the way I think we should do it. No one in the band has ever complained... Maybe I've said "tits" too many times and Tony will say, "I think you're getting too tits-orientated!", so I'll stop for a bit.

■ **By the end of 1976 Genesis had toured America and Europe and their next album, 'Wind And Wuthering', which was released in January 1977, reached number seven in the charts.**

● PHIL: We went to Holland to record 'Wind And Wuthering'. We stayed in this little house — all boys together. There were no ladies around. We just concentrated on the job in hand.

Most of the music was already written. I think you'll find that this is one of Tony's favourite albums, but then looking at the credits, it's no wonder!

It wasn't a hard album to write. Tony wrote several songs, Mike had a couple, and I chipped in here and there. I found that I wasn't writing much, which might have been caused by my marriage problems. I wasn't too involved with it; I did the best I could but I didn't feel that it was a true representation of what I wanted to do. Something wasn't quite right.

● TONY: If anyone ever asked me which was my favourite album, I'd say 'Wind And Wuthering'.

It's definitely the most musically complex of all our albums and it has a mysterious quality to it. I like most of the songs from this album. OK, I wrote a large proportion of them and I'm bound to feel closer to it in many ways, but I also liked the fact that this album didn't do as well as its predecessor. I suppose I'm just perverse.

'Trick Of The Tail' was a very easy album, you could hear it once, and know whether you were going to like it or not. 'Wind And Wuthering' was not like that. You needed to hear it several times before you could fully appreciate it.

'One For The Vine' — the longest track on the album — had taken over a year to develop. Whereas 'Afterglow' was written pretty much in the time it took to play it — it was a spontaneous piece, something I hadn't really done before.

● STEVE: I didn't feel that the songs that were included on 'Wind And Wuthering' were necessarily the best. For example, 'Spot The Pigeon' and 'Inside And Out', which turned up later on an EP, didn't get on to the album. Yet we included 'Wot Gorilla' which, to my mind, was a very inferior instrumental — a real doodle of an idea.

In fact there was a track of mine called 'Please Don't Touch' which was going to be on the album as the whole band were very keen on it. One day, in rehearsal, Phil said, "Can't get behind that", and we dropped it. I thought, "That's one of the best instrumentals that the band have done for a long time. Sod it, I'm going to do it myself".

I wrote another song I was very proud of called 'Hoping Love Will Last'. I felt the band were incapable of performing it and it was eventually recorded by Randy Crawford. I said to Phil one day, "I've written one of the best things I've ever done". And he said, "Solo material?" And I said, "Yeah". It was at that point that he knew how dissatisfied I was.

I felt that the band was starting to repeat itself; obviously there's always a certain amount of self-plagiarism but we weren't really exploring enough new areas.

The best stuff on 'Wind And Wuthering' was on side 2, but side 1 fell into clichés on certain tracks — predictable, swirling dynamics.

■ **Bill Bruford left to join UK while Genesis were recording 'Wind And Wuthering'. For their British and American tours early in 1977, they recruited Chester Thompson, who was born in Baltimore, Maryland, USA, in December 1948. He had played with Brother Jack McDuff, Frank Zappa, the Pointer Sisters and Weather Report.**

● BILL: I was very comfortable in Genesis. Much too comfortable in many ways. People tended to lump Yes, Genesis and King Crimson into the same bracket during the seventies and, having played in all three, I can say they were all incredibly unlike each other.

I think Genesis were good at writing pop songs, albeit very overblown ones at the beginning. They're much better at it now, their longevity has turned out to be their greatest strength. They were never the kind of tinkering band that King Crimson were. They were more traditional. I'm from the same public school background which I think throttles your emotional expression. Phil doesn't have that problem, he's a song and dance man. Mike and Tony have a much harder time trying to express what they are trying to say. As I do.

I always considered my time with Genesis as temporary, although the group were very friendly and never actually asked me to leave. It was just that I wanted to move on to something else.

I was rehearsing three songs with Rick Wakeman and John Wetton when a journalist at the *Melody Maker* decided that we were going to be the next supergroup. We denied all this, although Wetton and I later went on to form UK, which meant I was in three bands at the same time and I wasn't sure which one I wanted to be in. Finally I decided to go off and make my own record. In retrospect, I suppose I should have got on with my solo career instead of joining Genesis.

I think my stay with the band was coloured by my ambivalence about being a hired hand. Ninety per cent of musicians work like this but I had never done it before and it made me feel very underworked. I didn't have any creative input into Genesis. This meant I adopted a cynical attitude towards the band which I think they were really sweet to put up with. So I'd like to make a formal apology to the boys for being so gruesome while I was with them!

● PHIL: We read in *Melody Maker* that Bill was joining a group with Rick Wakeman and John Wetton. I rang him and said, "Are you with them or are you staying with us?" He said, "Ah, I meant to tell you about that!"

There was no grudge. Obviously, his time in the group was limited, because he wasn't writing with us. He helped us out of a hole, and I really enjoyed that particular line-up.

Then I went out and bought all these records, to try and find an English drummer. There was nobody suitable. I rang up Alphonso Johnson, who was our contact for musicians in America, and he found Chester for us.

I knew straight away that Chester was the right guy. He understood a lot of the material better than Bill had done.

Perhaps this was due to the fact that at that time I was very influenced by black music.

● CHESTER: I grew up in Baltimore. I was listening to R&B and there were these live shows that I could go to see at the Royal Theatre, which was exactly like the Apollo in Harlem. People like Sam Cooke, Little Stevie Wonder and Jackie Wilson would all tour together.

In 1970 I started out on the 'Chitterlin' Circuit' with Brother Jack McDuff. We toured all the small black clubs across the States.

CHRIS WALTER

San Diego, 1978.

I made $200 a week out of which I had to pay all my expenses. If you didn't work a whole week, you got paid less. That was the Chitterlin' Circuit — paying your dues.

I actually heard Genesis for the first time when I was with Weather Report. We used to play 'Trick Of The Tail' a lot on tour and I quite liked it although I didn't pay it a lot of attention.

However, I've got a real thing about playing music from other cultures, so when I was approached by Phil to join Genesis I thought it was the most perfect thing that could have come up at the time. I had never played anything 'properly British' before and I was really looking forward to it.

I had nine days rehearsal with the band and then we opened at the Rainbow Theatre in London. I got the worst review I could have possibly gotten — I've never had a review like that before or since.

Well, in the beginning, I thought the music was a bit stiff for my taste and the problem with those first rehearsals was having to remove some of the swing from my playing. These days they ask me to make it a bit funkier. I find that funny, they're beginning to sound almost like an R&B band.

On that very first British tour I did feel weird being in a group of English speaking people and not being able to understand one single word of what was said. That's the most alone I've ever felt in my life.

TONY: I think the emphasis that Chester gave to some of the old songs — a tendency to swing them a little bit — appealed to people a lot. It taught us something about our own music which I liked and live versions of some songs began to sound a lot better. 'Eleventh Earl Of Mar' is a good example — I thought it was much better live than it was on the album.

While Genesis were mixing a live album in the summer of 1977 Steve decided to leave.

STEVE: Once we'd shown that we could do it as a four piece, it all became too easy. We just played one 20,000-seater after another.

I started to ask myself, "What is it I really want?" I was suddenly writing more and more but the band incorporated less and less. I had an abundance of ideas but it didn't affect the overall ratio of Hackett songs to — let's be quite candid — Tony Banks songs.

I have a tremendous amount of respect for Tony, but there's no doubt about it, he was having the lion's share. I felt that after my first solo album it was like suddenly going back to school after being out at work.

I suddenly realised, "This is not the be-all and end-all of my career."

MIKE: It's always difficult if people start getting upset when some of their stuff is dropped.

Having just done an album all on his own Steve found it particularly frustrating.

I think he started to find working in the band with us too restricting.

● TONY: I'd always felt that Steve was with us temporarily. I think he felt that too and so it was really no surprise when he left. But I really enjoyed working with him, and I was very upset at some of the things that were said after he left which suggested that he felt a lot of antagonism towards me.

I didn't have any reciprocal bad feeling towards him, which worried me. Presumably I had been blind to things that had been bugging him a lot.

I don't think Steve and I ever got particularly close.

When he first joined, you could really see very little of the flesh on his face. He had big glasses, a full moustache and beard, heavy eyebrows and long hair.

By the time he left, he'd got rid of the glasses and the hair on his face. He was much more approachable and generally easier to get on with.

As a writer, he didn't contribute all that much. Ironically on 'Wind And Wuthering' he had contributed more than he had ever done. I felt that it was a bit strange that he left at that point, but then Pete's strongest contribution was probably his last album with us, 'The Lamb'.

● PHIL: Steve, unfortunately didn't write songs that appealed as much to everybody as Tony or Mike did but I thought his frustration at that time seemed unreasonable. He had a solo career, he could have pursued that. But, I don't think reason came into it. We were touring, I guess everyone was a bit tired. In the end, when 'Seconds Out' was being mixed, he just rang in and said, "My time's up." He could have stayed with us and done as many solo albums as he wanted.

After all the years it seemed funny that he was saying, "Listen, there's 40 minutes of music; therefore I want 10 minutes, because there's four people in the group."

It seemed a completely traditional way to approach things, especially coming from someone who knew very well how the band operated. We'd always worked on songs that motivated everybody, rather than, "I want a quarter of the album."

It was weird, I didn't feel emotional when he left. It had been very different when Pete left.

● CHESTER: Steve often wouldn't say anything, which always leads to problems. A band's got to be like a family. If somebody's not talking, then there's going to be tension.

■ **By the time their live double album 'Seconds Out' reached number four in the charts in October 1977, Mike, Tony and Phil were working on a new studio album with Mike playing all the guitar parts.**

● MIKE: 'And Then There Were Three' was a good album for me. When you get a big upheaval like that, it can be very frightening, but also very exciting.

At the time I was worrying so much about playing the lead guitar that parts of the album went by without me noticing them.

The minute I finished the album, I wanted to re-do all my parts. It was as if I had taken a crash course.

● TONY: 'And Then There Were Three' was a very even album, very consistent. It doesn't have the moments of magic like 'Foxtrot', 'The Lamb' or 'Wind And Wuthering', and is, therefore, slightly less adventurous.

● PHIL: It's not one of my favourite albums. I can't put my finger on why it isn't. I don't understand it at all.

● MIKE: We'd said to ourselves, "Let's keep some of the songs a bit shorter this time, so we can get slightly more variety." That made for a certain sort of album.

● TONY: I think 'Follow You Follow Me' is close to 'I Know What I Like', but it doesn't sound quite so eccentric.

We weren't thinking in terms of a single at all, at the time. We were just jamming on 'Follow You Follow Me' and suddenly realised that it would make a really good single. We had thought that so many times in the past but it had never proved to be the case.

As it happened, our producer Dave Hentschel didn't like the song at all and it almost got shelved. Hits are often flukes with us.

● MIKE: We were trying to prove ourselves. We were writing too much individually. The group songs weren't really group songs, in that they didn't come out of jams. They tended to be a bit of Phil, a bit of Tony and a bit of me.

● TONY: The 'Follow You Follow Me' jam worked like magic. The other jams didn't happen in the same way. It's the sort of thing we try for on every album — we had a lot of it on 'Trick Of The Tail'.

■ **'And Then There Were Three' was released in April 1978 and a single from it, 'Follow You Follow Me' put the group into the Top Ten for the first time, getting to number seven. For live work they again looked to America and found Daryl Stuermer, born in November 1952 in Milwaukee, Wisconsin, who had previously played with Sweetbottom, George Duke and Jean-Luc Ponty.**

● MIKE: We needed a bass guitarist to play

JILL FURMANOVSKY

□ *Daryl.*

guitar, or a lead guitarist who could play bass. Alphonso Johnson who is our contact for American musicians, came over. I had a session with him and, in the first fifteen minutes, realised that it was wrong — not because of him, but because we definitely needed a guitarist who could play bass. He suggested Daryl.

I went to America and saw a few guys. Pat Thrall — he was very good. Elliott Randall — I played some chords from 'Squonk', and he wasn't quite sure whether I wanted it funky or country or what. He could switch styles incredibly. And then Daryl came in. He'd actually learnt the songs. He played them right straight-away.

● DARYL: I come from Milwaukee which is just a middle-of-the-road town, but I like it. I moved back there after living in Los Angeles for five years. It's where the beer is, and Jerry Lee Lewis, and Liberace, and Al Jarreau.

I was going through a transitional period in 1978 because Jean-Luc Ponty was contemplating personnel changes. I was getting nothing out of the band anymore, and Ponty wasn't getting anything out of me.

I got a call from Ponty's manager who said, "A guy named Dick Fraser from Genesis is trying to call you. Here's his number." So I called him, and then found out that they wanted to audition me for Genesis.

I went to New York and auditioned with Mike. They had sent me four songs on a tape but in the end he only asked me to play 'Squonk' and 'Down And Out' before he said, "I think this is fine."

At the time, I didn't know much about Genesis. The only thing I'd heard by Genesis at the time was a song that Jean-Luc had played me. It was 'Squonk'. He'd said, "Listen to this drummer. The whole feel of the song is terrific!" He wanted to imitate that feel for a certain song of his own.

I heard Genesis had a great live show, but I didn't know what that meant. I thought that maybe they still wore costumes. I remember having seen Peter on a TV programme in America. He had his head shaved in the middle. They showed this clip of 'Supper's Ready' when Gabriel appeared in his flower costume.

I didn't get a good impression of them because I was more into jazz-fusion players. They were two totally different bands, I think — first with Peter and then with Phil.

I remember my wife saying, "Do you think you will fit in with Genesis?" I didn't know, I was certainly good enough technically but I wasn't sure if I could really feel this kind of music.

So, at first, I took the job somewhat reluctantly. I thought, "Well, I definitely want to get out of what I am doing. I'll give it a try." After playing in rehearsals, I thought, "This is great. I'm having to learn a lot of new sounds." It didn't come naturally at first but now I feel like I fit in. It just took a while; that's all.

At my first gig I saw a sign which read,

COURTESY CHARISMA

□ *Chester, Mike, Phil, Daryl, Tony, 1978.*

'Steve Hackett'. I don't think the audience knew that I wasn't him. Then, after they introduced me, the sign came down.

I was never given a hard time but I expected it. Steve definitely did have a following and an original style of playing.

It was put to me that I should try to duplicate some of Steve's parts because they were integral to the songs. But there were also certain sections where I was left to do what I liked.

I've duplicated some things, and on others I've put in my own little riffs. Some of the material was sounding dated anyway.

Later on I went with Phil to see Steve Hackett's solo show at the Roxy in Los Angeles, because I'd never met him, and I wanted to see his new band. I was just getting a drink, and someone came up to me and said, "Daryl Stuermer, you're my second favourite guitarist in the world!" I thought, "Oh, great. McLaughlin is his favourite." And this guy turned out to be Steve Hackett, it was really funny!

Phil was about the easiest one to get to know right away. Maybe because I understand him better. He's actually about 40% American! I got to know Mike next, because I worked closely with him at rehearsals. Tony's a much quieter person, but I didn't feel any tension. It was just a matter of taking time.

■ During 1978, Genesis played three American tours, a European festival tour (including the Knebworth Festival in August) and their first Japanese concerts. But early in 1979 they came close to disbanding when Phil's

marriage broke down. Tony and Mike each recorded solo albums — 'A Curious Feeling' and 'Smallcreep's Day' — which were released towards the end of the year.

● MIKE: We spent almost all of 1978 on the road. We had this crazy idea to do America in three short tours, rather than do one long tour.

What we didn't realise was that going there and back six times in a year made it seem much longer. The last tour tended to be in places where we hadn't made much of an impression, which was depressing for us.

● PHIL: I remember that on the eve of our '78 tour, my wife said to me, "We won't be together this time next year." I had just broken the news to her that we were going to be away all year. And we weren't. She could see it coming because she didn't like to be alone — and I was leaving her by herself a lot.

I remember it all very vividly. All rationality seemed to go out of the window then. I came back from the third American tour and the first night I slept in the spare room. It was that bad.

I just couldn't believe that this bloke that I'd brought in to decorate my house had actually gone off with my wife. Then I had to go away to Japan. Maybe I should have cancelled the tour.

But, no, I went to Japan, and I spent ten days drunk. I hated every minute of it. I couldn't sing and everyone was every concerned about my welfare, although there was nothing anyone could do about it.

When I came back, my wife and I decided to move to Vancouver. She wanted to be with her mum. So I said, "Right, we'll go to Vancouver. Let's sell the house."

I had dinner with Mike, Tony and Tony Smith, and I said, "Listen. If you don't mind coming to record in Vancouver, then we've still got a group. But if you can't, then this is the end.

So I went over there, looked around a few houses and thought, "OK, I'll do my album now and leave the group." Then it suddenly dawned on me that the marriage was no better than it had been in England.

I came back two months later and said, "OK, it's all over. What are we going to do?" They were right in the middle of their solo albums.

I made an album with Brand X and played some gigs with them. And we had a great time.

● TONY: It's in our natures to let each person cope with his own problems — our tendency is to stay away.

Mike and I felt very strongly that the best thing was to step back and let him sort it out. The last thing that Phil wanted was endless sympathy from us.

● MIKE: If I'd been in Phil's situation, I would have said, 'I'm sorry." The group would have seemed unimportant — your personal life has to come first.

● PHIL: Tony and Mike finished their albums, and we all gathered upstairs in my bedroom to do 'Duke'. I slept in the spare room for about six weeks. It was nice rehearsing under those circumstances — I would roll out of bed, get up and set up my drum kit. It was a very happy album. I played them 'In The Air Tonight', 'If Leaving Me Is Easy' and 'I Missed Again', which they rejected. So I kept them for my own album. But group songs like 'Behind The Lines' and 'Turn It On Again', were opportunities for me to get some funk into the group.

I'm glad the others didn't want to include 'In The Air', as I'm sure it wouldn't have ended up sounding the way I wanted it to.

● TONY: Suddenly the jams worked again. 'Duchess', 'Behind The Lines' and 'Turn It On Again' were written by us all together. I felt it was much more rewarding than just writing a lot of songs individually.

We couldn't have carried on with Mike and I writing the bulk of the material. There wouldn't have been much in it for Phil if we had carried on that way.

● MIKE: Every time we sat down and played a couple of chords together, we'd come up with something good. In the end, our writing became almost effortless.

● TONY: 'Behind The Lines' started off as a traditional Genesis song. Then, as it got going, this early Supremes feel crept in and the whole thing suddenly took on a completely different character.

● PHIL: I wrote some words to 'Behind The Lines' which I'm glad we didn't use. I started singing them, and everybody said, "You can't sing that." We were getting a lot of flak from the music press at the time, and I had written these pretty cynical lyrics which Tony and Mike were a bit embarrassed by.

● TONY: 'Duchess' is one of the best songs we've ever done. I'd almost rate it next after 'Supper's Ready'. It's very simple, but there's a lot of magic in five or six minutes. I like 'Please Don't Ask' very much but I'm not that keen on 'Misunderstanding.'

If it had never been brought out as a single I'd probably like it better. But when you take it out of context and make it 'The Single', in other words representing the whole album — which is what it was doing in the States — it just seemed rather insubstantial.

● PHIL: 'Misunderstanding' was meant to be about a girl meeting a boy. It was meant to be a song that anybody could listen to — not just Genesis fans. Whereas 'Please Don't Ask' was a very personal lyric.

LFI

□ *Phil and Peter, 1979.*

● TONY: I think Phil's singing really came together on Duke. He displayed himself as a real singer as opposed to just being a group singer who had just stepped up from the ranks. I felt that by the time we got to 'Duke', Phil was actually projecting his own personality into our songs. That's what a good singer should do.

■ **'Duke' was released in March 1980 and yielded the group's first major American hit 'Misunderstanding' which opened up a whole new audience for them. In Britain they played a 40-date tour of city halls, many of which they hadn't played for several years. Their growing profits enabled the group to build their own studio, The Farm, in Surrey, where they rehearsed and recorded 'Abacab'. They chose to produce themselves and used engineer Hugh Padgham who had worked with Phil on his first solo album, 'Face Value' which was released early in 1981.**

● PHIL: 'Abacab' was the first time that we really talked to each other. That's why I was so excited by 'Abacab' and that's why, as far as I'm concerned, the group almost starts there.

For instance there's a song called 'Me And Virgil' which eventually came out on the 'Paperlate' EP. Mike recorded his guitar solo for it, and he asked us what we thought of it. I was candid and said, "Really '67 acid stuff, man, I don't think we should use it.

He replied, "Do you know, I think you're right. Yes, you're right." He did it again and it was much better. But if I hadn't spoken my mind, we'd have used the first version.

'Duke' was very much a group album but 'Abacab' was literally just us, especially as we produced it ourselves.

● TONY: It was just a matter of courage to take it all into our own hands. We knew we could do it. We were already producing our own sounds. We knew what we wanted and we just needed to work with a competent engineer.

● MIKE: We managed to break a whole lot of taboos — little things, like turning a tape machine on and off, plugging things in and pulling them out!

Having our own studio took a lot of pressure off us. In the past, we'd book a studio and go in with nothing written which meant we were very conscious of how much it was all costing.

If we went to the loo, or had a long coffee break, and then couldn't think of anything to play for the next hour, we'd feel pretty miserable. Whereas, the idea of just being able to go and write in your own time is perfect.

● PHIL: There was a big difference between

working in our studio and going away to record an album as we no longer felt that we had to keep up a schedule.

We spent fourteen weeks making 'Abacab'. If something wasn't happening we'd stop and have a go at something else. Before, we'd have felt obliged to keep on trying to get it right.

● TONY: It took us longer than we'd planned as we had a few teething problems with the new studio and we also wrote far more than we used. We could have made a double album but decided against it.
We tried to change our appeal slightly by altering the arrangements. We managed to change the character without necessarily changing the original composition that much. It was nice to try and avoid the things that had become almost second nature to us.

It really made some songs sound much better. 'Abacab' itself wouldn't have been much good under the old approach. In 'Keep It Dark' the whole song structure is very different. We added some traditional Genesis ingredients to a song that was a new departure for us.

We didn't allow a single chord to creep into the song until the chorus. So when one comes it sounds ten times better than it would've done if you had heard one beforehand.

● MIKE: When we make an album, we're very insular. We don't give a shit about how people are going to react. Occasionally, you try something and you think, "God they're going to like this!" This album was different but I didn't see it as that different when we were doing it.

There's a lot of space on 'Abacab'. People tend to think of Genesis as a wall of sound but I think that's a thing of the past. This album is more the way we've sounded when we've been rehearsing.

● PHIL: It was my idea to get the Earth, Wind And Fire horn section on 'No Reply At All' and 'Paperlate'. We'd tried to simulate that brass sound on a couple of tracks on 'Duke'. I got to know Earth, Wind And Fire when I used them on my solo album and I was looking for a space for them on this album.

I was a bit worried that I was pushing a bit and putting my neck on the line if it didn't work. Tony had some reservations at the beginning but after I'd been over to America with the tape and put the horn parts on, he was happy with the way it sounded.

When we met Sting at the Secret Policeman's Ball, he said he really liked the 'Abacab' track. He thought it was really sixties. And I said, "Yes, it's funny that you should say that because the three bits in it are all sixties."

"There's the Easy Beats." and he said, "Yeah, Easy Beats. I know what you mean." I said, "And there's Booker T." And he said, "Yeah, I can see that." And then I said, "Stones." And he said, "Yeah, gotcha."

He had identified all three. It was like a quiz. So, maybe it is a sixties song. It's when we discovered the blues anyway.

JILL FURMANOVSKY

□ *Rome, 1982.*

● CHESTER: Genesis have got a certain...well I can't even say they've got a style that I'm familiar with, because every year it's been completely different.

I cracked up laughing in the tour rehearsals after 'Abacab' as they were talking about making it sound more funky, and I'd come all set to give it the old Genesis treatment. By making their songs swing a bit more they've kept on top of things — they don't sound the same now as they did five years ago.

● DARYL: As soon as Genesis started having hit singles some of the old fans didn't like it. You'd seen them turning up their noses when

Phil announced 'Follow You, Follow Me'. And I would think, "Open up! Just because it's sold well, doesn't mean it's a bad song."

Genesis found a whole new audience in America after a few hit singles. Everybody there had heard about the Genesis show, but they weren't selling nearly as many albums as they should have, considering they were regularly playing to 20,000 people.

I think their music is a little more pop orientated these days. They didn't sit down and say, "We're going to write a pop album" — it was a natural progression.

When you hear a song like 'Dodo', for instance, it almost has an old Genesis sound, but with a modern beat. I think the combination of old and new is now becoming more popular. And it's still keeping the old fans happy.

JILL FURMANOVSKY

REX FEATURES

REX FEATURES

Paris, 1983.

REX FEATURES

☐ *Pheel...*

REX FEATURES

☐ *Toni and...*

REX FEATURES

□ *...Miguel, 1983.*

REX FEATURES

□ *'Mama' video, 1983.*

CHRIS WALTER/PHOTOFEATURES

□ *Mike and Phil, 1984*

DAVE CORIO

1982.

1981-1984

'Abacab', released in September 1981, produced Top Ten singles on both sides of the Atlantic with the title track and 'No Reply At All'; an EP of extra songs, 'Paperlate', got to number eight in the British charts. This success enabled Genesis to sell out big stadia across America and their 1982 British tour attracted half a million ticket applications within two weeks of being announced.

A live double album 'Three Sides Live' was released in June 1982. In October 1982, Genesis were reunited with Peter Gabriel at a special one-off gig at the Milton Keynes Bowl in aid of the ethnically ambitious but financially disastrous WOMAD Festival (which Peter had been involved with). Sixty-thousand people turned up in the pouring rain.

Phil, Tony and Mike recorded solo albums — 'Hello, I Must Be Going', 'Acting Very Strange' and 'The Fugitive' respectively — before recording the fourteenth studio album as a group. Titled simply 'Genesis', it was released in October 1982, going instantly to the top of the British charts, making the American charts, and giving them their biggest British hit single with 'Mama'.

The following month they set out on a massive seventy-two date American tour and made their final appearance in 1984 with five British concerts in February.

● DARYL: When I first joined the band, I thought I would be on the records. They never actually talked to me about it, so after a while, I didn't think about it any more. It was hard to adjust to not being included on the albums, but I understand the reasons. The three of them basically write the songs in the studio and, if they got me in there, I would start adding my own ideas and become one of the song writers. They don't want to have any other song writers in the band. They had that before when they were five which resulted in clashes over the writing.

I have played on all three of their solo albums, which lets me know that they like what I'm doing.

REX FEATURES

□ *1982.*

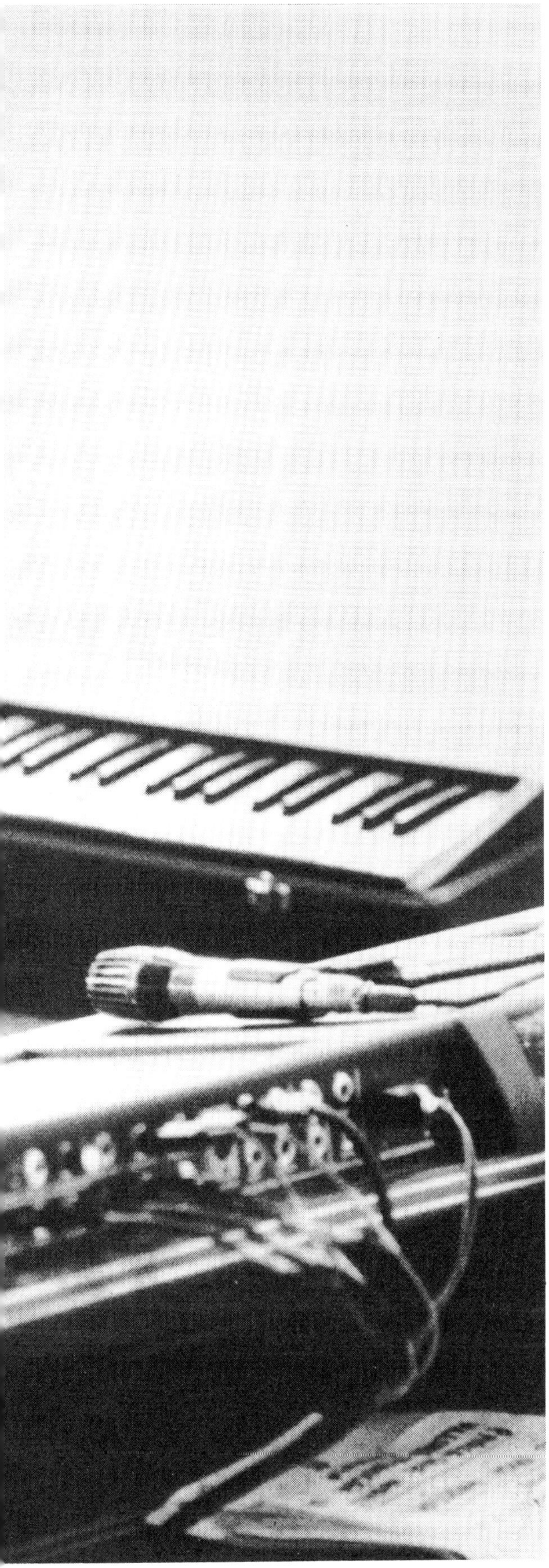

●CHESTER: The music's evolved a lot. A lot of old fans would argue and say they can't do this or that but I think it's a sign of maturity.

Some of their older stuff was really quite advanced for its time — some of it, I would even dare to say, was ahead of its time. I don't think they've compromised anything musically. They now say in five minutes what used to take them fifteen minutes.

At first, they used to say, "We're going to call you do to something on the album" — which never happened. It doesn't bother me because it wouldn't have sounded like Genesis. I mean, it's a pretty unique combination, it's as if there's some magic which happens when the three of them get together.

JILL FURMANOVSKY

●TONY: I think our playing is very unselfconscious with just the three of us. Anyone else would make us play a little differently and cause us to worry about bum notes.

When the three of us play together it's almost like being on your own, you don't feel inhibited and can just jam along. People respond in a different way if there are other people around. You start to perform when you shouldn't.

In some groups, there are one or two leading lights, and some of the other members probably get a bit frustrated because they feel they're probably contributing just as much but don't get the credit. It's never been a factor with us.

I think anyone in this business must have something of an ego. It's important to gratify that.

First and foremost in my mind is the music; once we finish one album, I'm thinking about the next. Touring is just something that comes in between. The road is part of my life, but it's the least important part of my career.

I think you have to be very motivated — it's the only reason for all the touring. And yet playing live is probably what keeps you fresh.

I find it very exciting that people want to hear my music — whether in Hong Kong or

Barnstaple. I feel it's a unifying force — something that brings people together, rather than pushes them apart — which I'm definitely in favour of.

My contribution is definitely in the writing and recording areas. I play OK on stage, but I don't contribute that much to the visual performance of the group.

I respond to an audience, but very much inside myself. People always say, "He never smiles", or "He never does anything." But it really helps me to know an audience is enjoying our show. There's no doubt that if you want a good concert, the best thing is to go ecstatic after the first number, whatever it sounded like, and you'll get a much better performance. It sounds absurd, but as a performer I know that an audience's reaction makes an awful lot of difference.

We made changes in the recent albums to keep our interest alive. We don't want to become complacent. We probably could have gone on doing 'Cinema Show' and other old favourites for a long, long time and still have kept big audiences. This way we carry on enjoying it.

People say, "Genesis are always the same" — I don't see that. I think we are very different from track to track and album to album. At one moment we may sound a bit like Stevie Wonder, and the next moment more like Ultravox. We are just very diverse. I'm sometimes amazed at how little groups break out of their particular areas. I'd find that very restricting and some guys have been doing the same things for about five or six years.

We've been such a slow growing band but we have never stopped growing since the moment we started. Almost every album has sold more than its predecessor. And there can't be many groups who've managed to do that over ten or eleven years.

This is the contemporary rock music era. We're not talking about music that's supposed to be liked twenty years from now. It's supposed to be liked here and now. We don't claim to be more esoteric than that.

I don't try to live out anybody else's ideas of what a rock and roll lifestyle should be like. I just do it my way. We do well out of the band. We make more than enough money now. I can't spend masses of money like some people can. It doesn't suit me. I like a nice house — and I'll spend money on that. That's the main draw on my income. I definitely feel overprivileged; I can't avoid that, because I have socialist tendencies.

●MIKE: After all these bloody albums you suddenly realise that the years are ticking by. For so long, I think, the quality of our lives has just been forgotten — we've had to let go, in order to get that tour done or finish that album off in time. There are so many things that I would like to do — production, writing for other people, films — and unless I leave myself time they will never happen. However, my solo albums mean I've got more energy for Genesis than I have had for a long time.

JILL FURMANOVSKY

COURTESY CHARISMA

Now, we leave a bit more time open, and we don't plan ourselves so tightly.

If you think about it, having been a professional musician for a dozen years or so, one album a year isn't enough for the amount of material you've amassed. The solo albums provide an outlet and the group is stronger as a result because we don't have to impose stuff on each other.

It seems an odd thing to say, but if we didn't get on, were never even friendly and had separate dressing-rooms, it wouldn't matter. I wouldn't enjoy it as much, but we could still survive just on the strength of the music. That's the main thing.

Having said all this, the fact that we do get on better now, makes the group even more enjoyable.

As people we've been getting on much better over the last two or three years. We've opened up to each other's wishes.

I suppose I'm very selfish in a way — as long as it suits me, I don't make any noise.

The personnel changes helped to give us new challenges, but in other ways they became a hindrance. Because it was 'the first album without Peter' and then 'the first album without Steve'. If we hadn't had those problems we might have got to where we are now sooner.

After Peter left we felt we had to prove ourselves as writers. We felt underrated. We've reached the end of that era now and we've gone back to writing songs as a group.

The reason we're three now is that as the five of us developed there just wasn't room to fit us all in.

When Pete left and we were down to four, there was a feeling of relief amongst us all because there was suddenly more room. Then after a while, even four seemed too many — too much friction, too many ideas — and then we were down to three. And then three seemed too...no, three is a good number! — for the time being!

● PHIL: When Peter saw us at Hammersmith just after I started singing, he said, "You sing 'Supper's Ready' and 'Carpet Crawlers' better than I do, but you'll never sing them like I do." It's the notes that really get me going. I think he's right about that. I know I sing it better than he sings it, but he sings it with more understanding.

I've always been a firm believer in the sound of the word, rather than what that word means. 'Follow You, Follow Me' and 'Alone Again Tonight', for instance, are two songs of Mike's. In them he's trying to say "I love you", but the way he says "I love you" is "I love you, darling", as opposed to "Shit, I miss you". I really can't get behind those lyrics.

It's very hard to sing someone else's words. We were listening to some of our old live tapes, and 'bread bin' was in one of the lyrics; now, how do you sing 'bread bin?'. Or how do you sing 'undinal', which is in 'Firth Of Fifth"?

I know exactly how the band operates, it

JILL FURMANOVSKY

☐ *Kate Rutherford, Benjamin Banks and Phil Collins, Edinburgh, 1980.*

operates in the way it always has. We wouldn't have it any other way. When we were making 'Abacab', and I said, "That isn't quite right. Why don't we do this?", or "Let's not do that. We've done that," my words were given a bit more weight.

I had never finished writing a song for the group before 'Misunderstanding' which was our first big hit in America. Suddenly my album came out and I was seen as a bit of a writer, which Tony and Mike appreciated, I think.

So now, as a writer, I'm up with Tony and Mike, who were the two who wrote what people have always described as typical Genesis music.

I was there to say, "How about this there, how about that there?" Maybe I made it more palatable, maybe I took it away from those self-conscious, grandiose settings by putting a bit of funk rhythm into it. That was my strength up to 'Misunderstanding'. Now we are all writers.

Genesis is just part of what I do, I have my solo albums and my production work with other people. The only reason I play with the group is because I really want to. I've realised that there's no point in doing anything which is supposed to be an expression of yourself unless it's a genuine one. The day you stop being honest is the day you should pack it in altogether.

I can tell when Tony really likes something. He'll never say to me, "You played great tonight, or you sang great tonight." He just won't tell me what I did wrong.

I've always thought of Mike as midway between me and Tony. I'm much more of a rational person than Tony or Mike. Although Tony is Mr. Logic — by definition, he is a logical person! I'm not trying to do him down, because he's wonderful, you know!

I'm very paranoid about people seeing through me. I feel that when I'm on stage in front of 10,000-20,000 people, they will suss if I'm a schmuck.

You can only hope that people will look at you and say, "This guy's genuine; this guy's not mucking about."

The group is a family now. I remember when we were looking for singers and a bloke walked into the room — our first thoughts were "Is he going to be able to become part of the family?"

When you know each other so well, and suddenly someone else comes in, it's very hard to see them as one of us. I see it cosmically as well — 'Mother Ship!' You can't contain everybody. Maybe if Steve and Pete hadn't quit, maybe one of us would have left. After Peter left, we could never convince people that Genesis was a five-piece writing group. When you lose one member, you lose a fifth of the whole.

Providing the majority of members are still the original members, you're in business, you've got whatever it is — the chemistry, the identifiable sound or style — it's still there.

When Steve left, there were still the three of us — and I consider myself to be an original member. I 'm still called the new boy, but I've been there eleven years■

REX FEATURES

ALBUMS

From Genesis To Revelation — March 1969. (Decca SKL4990). Re-released as Genesis Roots 1976.

Trespass — October 1970 (Charisma CAS1020)

Nursery Cryme — November 1971 (Charisma CAS1052)

Foxtrot — October 1972 (Charisma CAS1058)

Genesis Live — June 1973 (Charisma CLASS1)

Selling England By The Pound — October 1973 (Charisma CAS1074)

The Lamb Lies Down On Broadway — November 1974 (Charisma CGS101)

A Trick Of The Tail — February 1976 (Charisma CDS4001)

Wind And Wuthering — December 1976 (Charisma CDS4005)

Seconds Out — October 1977 (Charisma GE2001)

And Then There Were Three — April 1978 (Charisma CDS4010)

Duke — March 1980 (Charisma CBR101)

Abacab — September 1981 (Charisma CBR102)

Three Sides Live — June 1982 (Charisma GE1002)

Genesis — October 1983 (Charisma GENLP1)

PERSONNEL

January 1967-March 1968 — Tony Banks, Peter Gabriel, Anthony Phillips, Mike Rutherford, Chris Stewart.

June 1968-August 1969 — Tony Banks, Peter Gabriel, Anthony Phillips, Mike Rutherford, John Silver.

September 1969-July 1970 — Tony Banks, Peter Gabriel, John Mayhew, Anthony Phillips, Mike Rutherford.

August 1970-February 1971 — Tony Banks, Mick Barnard, Phil Collins, Peter Gabriel, Mike Rutherford.

February 1971-May 1975 — Tony Banks, Phil Collins, Peter Gabriel, Steve Hackett, Mike Rutherford.

May 1975-March 1976 — Tony Banks, Phil Collins, Steve Hackett, Mike Rutherford.

March 1976-November 1976 — Tony Banks, Bill Bruford, Phil Collins, Steve Hackett, Mike Rutherford.

December 1976-June 1977 — Tony Banks, Phil Collins, Steve Hackett, Mike Rutherford, Chester Thompson.

June 1977-November 1977 — Tony Banks, Phil Collins, Mike Rutherford.

December 1977 to the present — Tony Banks, Phil Collins, Mike Rutherford, Daryl Stuermer, Chester Thompson.